WHY DO I SAY "YES" WHEN I NEED TO SAY "NO"?

Michelle McKinney Hammond

HARVEST HOUSE™ PUBLISHERS

EUGENE, OREGON

Cover by Koechel Peterson & Associates, Minneapolis, Minnesota

Published in association with the literary agency of Alive Communications, Inc., 7680 Goddard Street, Suite 200, Colorado Springs, CO 80920

WHY DO I SAY "YES" WHEN I NEED TO SAY "NO"?

Formerly published as *The Genius of Temptation*
Copyright © 2002, 1998 by Michelle McKinney Hammond
Published by Harvest House Publishers
Eugene, Oregon 97402

Library of Congress Cataloging-in-Publication Data
McKinney Hammond, Michelle, 1957–
   [Genius of temptation]
   Why do I say "yes," when I need to say "no"? / Michelle McKinney Hammond
      p. cm.
   Originally published: The genius of temptation. c1998.
   Includes bibliographical references.
   ISBN 0-7369-0869-2
      1. Temptation. 2. Spiritual life—Christianity. I. Title.
BT725.M37 2002
241'.3—dc21   2001051701

Printed in the United States of America

02   03   04   05   06   07   08   09   10   / BC-CF /   10   9   8   7   6   5   4   3   2

Acknowledgments

THERE are so many men of God who have influenced my life through their messages, directly or indirectly, over the years. I feel this book is the fruit of the seeds they planted while teaching me the deep and hidden mysteries of God. Thank you for saying things that made me say, "Hmmm," while provoking me to stretch beyond where I had grown content.

Bishop Luther Blackwell
Pastor Joel Brooks Jr.
Pastor Aaron Fruh
Dr. Richard D. Hinton
Bishop T.D. Jakes
Noel Jones
Bishop Carlos Malone
Curtis Miller

Mike Murdock
Pastor Fiifi Pentsil
Pastor Bob Phillips
Charles Stanley
Chuck Swindoll
Kenneth Ulmer
Frank Wilson
Rev. Tony Williams

A very special thank-you to Bill Jensen, who planted the seed, asked me to write this book, watered it, and nourished this author into producing fruit. LaRae, thanks for breathing new life into what could have been old news (smile). Steve Miller, you are great!

Thank you to Bob Jr., Carolyn, Betty, and...oh, all the family at Harvest House. You are truly family at this point. May we grow old together. Words cannot express how wonderful all of you are. You make me want to give my best for you.

CONTENTS

Foreword

HERE IS A BOOK THAT REMINDS US that behind the trap is the trapper; behind the lie is the liar. It reminds us the good news is that God has a wonderful plan for your life, but the bad news is that Satan has a *destructive* plan for your life.

Michelle McKinney Hammond knows both the power of temptation and the grace that God can give us to overcome it. She writes with a realistic grasp of how often we fool ourselves by *wanting* to be tempted; we hesitate when we should run and play when we should fight. At the end of the day, we are deceitful creatures indeed!

I've known Michelle McKinney Hammond for many years and have seen how God has steadily worked in her life to bring her to a point of contentment with who she is as a Christian woman. Her road has not always been easy, and like many of us, she has learned through her own personal struggles.

The moment you begin to read this book you will know that God has graciously gifted Michelle as a writer, a woman who can speak with a candor and perception. You will come away with a better understanding of your weaknesses, and best of all, you will be better able to recognize Satan's strategy in the many choices you face daily.

I commend this book to all who are interested in not repeating the same cycle of bondage to the lures of the devil. You will see yourself in these pages, but you will also see God's grace and power.

Enjoy this book. But above all, learn from it. You will be glad you did.

—Dr. Erwin Lutzer
Senior Pastor, Moody Church

FROM THE BEGINNING

TAKE ME IN, TENDER WOMAN. TAKE ME IN, for goodness' sake.
Take me in, tender woman,' sighed the snake." This popular
song of the 1960s, sung by the late Oscar Brown, Jr., spun a
woeful tale of an unassuming woman who allowed herself to
be sucked in by the smooth conversation of a wily snake. She
happened to stumble upon him as he lay frozen in the snow,
and his piteous cries for help wiped out her sound reasoning
that his bite could be lethal if she took him into her home. He
reassured her that his gratitude would override his nature to
bite, and being the kind sort that she was, she took the snake
in to be warmed by the fire. Well, the rest of the story is predictable enough. Fully recovered, the snake bit the woman,
and when she reminded him of his promise not to strike at

her, he calmly countered, "You knew I was a snake when you took me in." (Sounds like a player to me!)

Indeed he was a snake, yet he had painted himself as something else—a helpless frozen being whose character had been transformed by the hardship he had suffered. He knew a naïve victim when he saw one. He knew exactly what to say and what to leave to supposition. This is the genius of temptation at work. After all, it is the great "Suppose..." that gets most of us in trouble.

"I didn't know..." "I never thought..." and "It just...happened" are the famous last words heard repeatedly by the victims of a fall that has been craftily designed by another infamous snake, Satan himself.

Since the beginning of time, a snake has always been a snake. His character remains true—flexible, calculating, and deadly. With this knowledge confirmed as fact, man has continued to have conversations with the snake for generations to the same end. Echoes of dismay have resounded through the ages, for the seduction of the snake has continued to ensnare all who stop to consider his offerings. How does he continue to wreak havoc in the lives of those who seemingly recognize him for what he is yet fail to shun his entreaties?

The answer is simple: Snakes love to lure their victims into the shadows—the shadows of ignorance, where curiosity and naïveté grow wild and free. Where perversions of the truth roam unbridled and where feelings of entitlement wind like vines around the hearts of those teetering on the precipice of rebellion. This is where the snake works best and paints his greatest illusions. And this is where men stumble and fall, unable to see their way clearly.

Perhaps you recognize a snake when you see one, but the Bible urges us to not be ignorant of his devices. Perhaps you are one who sees the trap, but still gets sucked in by its allure. You find yourself saying yes when every other instinct within you screams *no*. The regret after the deed is done is overwhelming as you grope for the answer to why you allowed yourself to be seduced. Hopefully this book will shed some light on your path and help you to avoid the snares of temptation.

1

THE DECEIVER
AND THE DECEIVED

"The heart is deceitful above all things, and desperately wicked: who can know it?"

JEREMIAH 17:9 KJV

DOWN THROUGH THE CENTURIES, the world has lauded athletes, actors, and others who have mastered a specific craft or skill, but I have no recollection of any man or woman who was praised publicly for his or her mastery over sin. As a matter of fact, I remember that back in my childhood days someone who followed the rules to the letter was labeled a "Goody Two-Shoes." And Goody Two-Shoes was not a flattering nickname. It screamed of someone who was uptight, not with it, a spoiler of fun, a "chicken" who would spill the beans and ruin the fun for everyone else who wanted to somehow secretly defy authority and break the rules. You were "big stuff" and others admired you if you could "get away with murder"—that is, break the rules without getting caught. But the fact is, these children who went against authority grew up and experienced major problems as adults. And these problems could, in most cases, be traced back to the habits they formed in their early disobedience. Right and wrong have become difficult to define in today's society. "It's your thing; do what you wanna do," is the mantra of the day Shifting mores, numbed consciences, and the newly introduced idea of "political correctness" that urges us to be more tolerant of others' "alternative choices" have caused many of our personal values to become seriously misplaced.

Though being "politically correct" sounds very nice and accommodating to the masses, one major opinion has been overlooked—that of God Himself. After all, He is watching us, and not "from a distance" as a popular song suggests. In the face of changing times and opinions, His standard for living a righteous and holy life remains constant. None of His rules have been relaxed to accommodate what we view as present-day dilemmas that should be taken into consideration. Yet many people, against their better judgment, choose to defy the Word of God for what they see as a moment of harmless fulfillment, ignoring the ever-present bottom line and powerful truth that "there is a way that seems right to a man, but in the end it leads to death" (Proverbs 14:12 NIV).

What is so delectable and tantalizing about breaking the rules? Why do people dare to dance so close to the fire even when they know that fire burns? What makes people push the envelope, gambling with their reputations, possessions, and the lives of their loved ones? Deception—clear and simple. The pretext of rationalizing that what others don't know won't hurt them. But that theory is loaded with false promise. Disobedience to God's law makes you a slave— either to the consequences of the violation if you're discovered by others, or to the lie itself if you do manage to "get away with it." So what is it exactly that makes stepping over the line worth the risk? It's the beauty, the appeal, the allure of deception's first cousin...temptation.

Remember the Lone Ranger? I loved it when he came racing up on his horse to save the day. The intended victim—now the rescued—would look off into the distance as the Lone Ranger rode toward the horizon, saying in a voice filled with wonder, "Who was that masked man?" And so it is with Temptation, who—unlike the Lone Ranger—pushes us toward disaster. As soon as a spot of vulnerability shows up on our foreheads, Temptation stands by waiting for the pimple to burst. And he keeps picking at it and picking at it until it's good and infected, sure to leave a scar, and then *poof!* He's gone as soon as the damage is done. And we stand there scratching our heads and wondering how we ever got into this mess.

The answer is really quite simple: "When man is beguiled and lured by his own desire, then passion conceives, gives birth to, breeds, or produces death" (James 1:14-15, a compilation of the AMP, TCNT, NEB, and Beck translations).[1] And the masked man named Temptation is off and running, leaving disaster in his wake.

"Why me?" we often cry. And the answer comes back, "Why not you? You were ripe for the picking. You had a desire that Temptation was happy to fill."

The Tempter Unmasked

The lament has been sung, "The tempter stalks about me like a lion, searching the slightest scent of blood. For when the skin of my resistance is broken he moves in quickly to deepen the cut." That about sums it up. The Word of God tells us that we should "be sober, be vigilant; because your adversary the devil, as a roaring lion, walketh about, seeking whom he *may* devour" (1 Peter 5:8 KJV, emphasis added). Who is that masked man who goes by the name of Temptation? A serpent more

subtle than all existing creatures, a roaming lion, an angel of
light...each description grows more intriguing than the last. So
what would we write if we were designing a "Most Wanted"
poster for this most notorious felon? How would we describe
him? We couldn't write down his specific height or weight
because we know him to be a chameleon.

Temptation metamorphoses to become whatever is most
fitting to accomplish his task. He reminds me of the hero in
an old movie, *Thief of Hearts*. The hero was a thief who spe-
cialized in robbing rich people's homes. One night, upon
breaking into yet another home, he became enamored with
a portrait of one of his victims and decided to steal her diary
as well. This he studied meticulously until he had memorized
all of her fantasies. On that note, he proceeded to enter her
life and fulfill all of her dreams. The woman was married, but
her husband was not fulfilling all of her secret desires, so off
she went with the thief. Get the picture? "But how do I recognize the 'thief' in my own life?" you may ask. As I've said
time and time again, our elusive friend Temptation is not into
red suits, as rumored.

Profiles in Deceit

Perhaps we would get somewhere if we studied his list of
aliases. Temptation is also known in the King James Version
of the Bible as Lucifer (Isaiah 14:12-14), the Devil and Satan
(Revelation 12:9), Beelzebub (Matthew 10:25; 12:24), Belial
(2 Corinthians 6:15), our adversary (1 Peter 5:8-9), a dragon
(Revelation 12:3-12), a serpent (2 Corinthians 11:3), the god
of this world (2 Corinthians 4:4), the prince of this world
(John 12:31), the prince of the power of the air (Ephesians
2:2), the accuser of our brethren (Revelation 12:10), the
deceiver of the whole world (see Revelation 12:9), the enemy
(Matthew 13:39), and that wicked one (1 John 5:18).

Some of these names are not very flattering, but they certainly allude to Temptation's character traits if we take a closer look. For example, take Beelzebub, a name that means "lord of the flies." Flies are one of the filthiest species known to man. They are one of the main carriers of bacteria and disease. Every function of their body contributes to spreading this filth, even eating. They feed on filth and distribute the residue wherever they land. Like a fly, Satan loves to smear us in sin. He enjoys filth, and he loves covering us in it. He thrives on dropping infectious lies, fears, and emotions into our lives and watching them fester into cancerous infirmities—either spiritually, emotionally, or physically. The method doesn't matter as long as the end result is the same—death.

What is it about serpents? Some have the ability to swallow their prey whole, while others slowly squeeze the life out of their victims. Some slither along indistinguishable to the undiscerning eye because they blend in with the scenery. But when a serpent decides to strike suddenly, his sting is deadly. Subtle, crafty, and hypnotic, he places his victim under his spell. Paralyzed with fear and lacking quick enough reflexes to escape, the victim becomes infected with the serpent's lethal poison before he or she even knows what happened. And Satan is the ultimate master of lulling us into our comfort zone before he makes his move.

Why poison? Why not just a quick and painless death if that's all he wants? Let us consider the mind of one who is filled with hatred and loathing for his victim. Imagine the delight of watching the object of his vengeance writhing in slow, painful deterioration. I don't believe that the authors of the books of the Bible just haphazardly chose names to symbolize Satan's character. The names were chosen to reflect who Satan really is and to let us know of his methods of operation. Snakes spread their poison in order to do three things—avoid being preyed upon, protect their resources, and capture their prey. Of course Satan wants to keep his followers. He doesn't want a bunch of powerful, victorious Christians running around converting his charges. He most certainly doesn't want those in high and powerful places to see the light and start using their influence to spread the gospel. But most of all, Satan loves to use his sting to injure those who love God and watch his poison do its terrible work in a child of God.

For an example of this, turn to the book of Ruth and read about poor Naomi. Naomi's name meant "pleasant and beautiful," but she changed it to Mara, which meant "bitter," because she thought the Lord had dealt bitterly with her. I have watched many today stuck in the quagmire of bitterness toward God. This bitterness works as pure, unadulterated poison. How can we get anywhere if we are angry and not speaking to the only One who can do something about our lives? If we cut ourselves off from the hand that feeds us, how do we eat? My mother used to call it "cutting off your nose to spite your face." Yet our beguiling serpent friend has found the poison of bitterness most effective in ruining the lives of many.

Bitterness, disappointment, and unforgiveness do not only affect the soul. They can also affect the body in some cases, generating sickness and disease. Oh, the transformation that takes place in the countenance and physique of those who have allowed this poison to ravage their heart! They take on a hard look, a darkness surrounds them, and a spirit of rejection trails them, shooing away anyone who might be interested in lending assistance. This further heightens their case against God. They can't understand why nothing ever works out for them, and yet the poison continues to seep silently through their bloodstream, robbing them of the hope they need to rise to the place of victory. And poor God is named as the culprit. How convenient.

I have been treated unfairly by others in life. I've been falsely accused and used. Evil has been spoken of my good intentions and actions, and I've laid on my bed in tears, asking God why He would ever allow such things to happen to me. After all, I work so hard for Him! I am ever mindful of doing the right thing. And He so gently asks me, if His only begotten Son was abused and offended, how do I intend to escape this same type of treatment? Intellectually I understand this, but while I'm still smarting from the fresh sting of the serpent, that answer brings me no peace. I nurse and rehearse what happened and fail to see the reason in the attack. And then I ask God the same question I've asked Him several times before: "How did Joseph ever get over what his brothers did to him? How did he ever get over what Potiphar's wife did to him? How did he ever forgive the chief butler for forgetting him after he had so miraculously helped him? How could he be so gracious to these people after what they did to him?" And God replies, "He accepted my grace." Such a simple thing, yet so difficult to do because the more we stare at the offense instead of the one standing behind the offender, the more we cut off the IV—if you will—of God's grace. We slap away the hand that offers the Balm of Gilead, which is meant to soothe the hurt and help us see clearly that the attack was not against us personally. Rather, it was against our God-ordained purpose. You're in trouble if your road is consistently too smooth, my brother or sister. A smooth road means you are no threat to the kingdom of darkness. There is not enough spiritual movement in your life to catch the eye of the snake.

As a Roaring Lion

But let's move on to the lion. Lions are carnivorous beasts. The word *carnivore* tells us a lot. Broken down to the root, *carnis* means "flesh," while *vorare* means "to eat." "To eat flesh"—I would say that description is rather precise. Satan feeds upon the needs of our flesh. "The lust of the flesh" is a powerful thing. Its scent attracts Satan—aka Temptation—who "as a roaring lion, walketh about, seeking whom he may devour" (1 Peter 5:8 KJV). Lions move undercover, hunting in the darkness of the night. They stalk their victims in groups (thus the need for demon cronies). Usually one lion drives the prey toward the other lions, who lie in wait. The adult male of the pride often takes no major role in the hunt, but nevertheless will claim his portion of the kill. Now, ain't that just like the devil?

Satan is not omnipotent, so he makes others do his dirty work for him while he claims all the credit and the spoils. And like the lions in the hit movie *The Ghost and the Darkness,* Satan grows bolder when he sniffs the subtle fragrance of Fear. Fear is one of his best friends. It paralyzes his targets, making them prime for pouncing. Highly intelligent, Satan has no problem watching, circling, and waiting until the opportune time arrives to move in for the kill. And when he does, he is merciless.

What then of dragons? A great mystery surrounds dragons. Did they really ever exist? Many people ask the same question about Satan. Is he a mythological character with horns and a pitchfork who resides in some hot corner in the center of the earth? Or is he more real and sinister than we would care to admit? Great and terrible dragons held many a storybook princess ransom, and defeated many a dashing storybook knight with one whiff of fiery breath. Now, that's some serious halitosis! Fire devoured all who stood in opposition to the dragon as he shielded his captured prize beneath his awesome wings.

What an interesting flip side of an altogether different picture of the Lord Himself, who keeps us safe beneath the shadow of His wings. Here instead is a creature that represents danger instead of safety, fear instead of peace. The breath of Satan destroys everything within its path. It pays no

heed to guilty or innocent; in his mind, all are worthy of per-
ishing. He is fed by the fuel of his own inner inferno, his
loathing for all that God loves and treasures, and his hatred
for God Himself. The poison that he is so anxious to spread
is the same poison that motivates his every move. Every time
Satan shakes his puny fist at God, he is determined not to be
empty-handed. He must wave a prize that he's plucked from
God's own trophy case, as if wielding an arrow he knows is
sure to pierce the heart of The One Who Loves Us Most. And
so he holds another destroyed soul aloft, crowing with
delight.

This elusive thief, this creature who works beneath the
cloak of mortal weaknesses and who seems to be irrepress-
ible, has been stumping the keenest minds for generations.
How does he do what he does? How is it that we never seem
to have a hint of warning that he is in the vicinity? How many
have been left sitting among the ruins of their life, wondering
what really happened? When did it all start going wrong?
How were they blindsided like this?

Satan is the most dangerous type of criminal. He is a serial
killer who seemingly leaves no trace of evidence behind that
implicates him as the murderer. He is on a rampage, making
war against the saints on a global level. In order to escape
being part of the carnage, we must take a closer look at how
he selects his victims.

The Open Door

Ever since I gave my heart to the Lord, I have periodically
had the same dream. I dream that robbers have found their
way into my home. Upon inspecting the door I presumed I
had locked, I discover that I actually hadn't. Instead I had left
it standing barely open, giving easy access to my unwelcome
intruders. I pursue them, trying to pull out of their hands the
things they are stealing, but they ignore my protests and

continue taking things as if they have the right to them. In time I came to learn that this dream is God's way of letting me know that I have a door open in my life that could allow Satan to take advantage of me. Now, upon awaking from this dream, I pray right away and ask God to reveal which door I have left open for the enemy's attack. He is always faithful to show me, and I always slam it shut with a vengeance.

Jesus Himself said, "When the unclean spirit is gone out of a man, he walketh through dry places, seeking rest; and finding none, he saith, I will return unto my house whence I came out. And when he cometh, he findeth it swept and garnished. Then goeth he, and taketh to him seven other spirits more wicked than himself; and they enter in, and dwell there: and the last state of that man is worse than the first" (Luke 11:24-26 KJV). Now tell me, why do people assume that Jesus is not speaking to the church here? The big hint is, "When the unclean spirit is gone out of a man." Nothing else can make this occur, save the cleansing that takes place through the blood of Jesus Christ. So where does that leave us with the rest of this story?

The moment we say "I do" to Christ, the devil does not pack his bags peacefully and give up on us forever. As he did when he was finished trying to tempt Jesus in the wilderness, he withdraws and waits for a more opportune time to begin his next sin crusade. Let's liken this parable to a few modern-day examples. Ever been on a diet? Ever notice that when your diet is over you end up eating double the amount of food, as if you're making up for lost time? How many people can testify that they gained back twice the weight they lost? Get the picture? Likewise, people who quit smoking and then start again end up smoking more than they did before they quit. What is happening here?

Now take another look at Luke 11:24-26. Salvation is a free gift. Deliverance, freedom from bondage, and victorious living all cost something. They cost us a lifetime of self-denial and obedience to the Word of God and the leading of the Holy Spirit. When you decide to ignore God's Word and the Holy Spirit, you are opening the door for trouble to enter. Why do people open the door to dangerous strangers? Because they are deceived into thinking that their visitor is harmless. Samson was deceived into thinking he could continue in blatant sin and still receive God's help when he was attacked by his enemies. Saul was deceived into thinking he was the one true king of Israel and could do as he pleased. David was deceived into thinking he could kill Uriah and keep his dalliance with Bathsheba under wraps.

The Price of Entertaining Sin

Lot's wife was deceived into thinking it was perfectly harmless for her to look back as they were fleeing Sodom. Even after receiving explicit directions from the Angel of the Lord, she just had to sneak a peek. What was she thinking? "Gee, we just got settled! I'm so sick of moving...especially when I'd just gotten our house decorated the way I like it. I can't believe I had to leave my china and my fabulous dinette set, not to speak of all the clothes I just got back from the tailor. I bet I can probably see the house from here; I sure am going to miss it. Oh, what the heck? What would it hurt if I just snuck one quick peek? It couldn't be that bad—after all, aren't I giving up enough?" And on that note she swiveled around to take one last look for posterity and immediately turned into a pillar of salt. How many of us reach back to indulge in one seemingly harmless bad habit, then find ourselves immediately bound in the past, unable to move on, unable to move past where we presently are? That's what that pillar of salt symbolizes to me. Being stuck, unable to make progress or reach our dreams.

I once heard a minister say that when you begin to back-slide, you will revisit the last thing you left behind and proceed backward in consecutive order. What makes any of us think we can get away with anything God has asked us not to do without suffering the consequences? The voices of Deception and Temptation urge us on, encouraging us to test the indulgence of our Heavenly Father. Whether the indulgence be a lie or the homosexual lifestyle, our inclination is to decide, "I can't help it, and God will love me anyway." This is a dangerous thought process. Sin—no matter what kind it is—is still sin to God. The only person who has the right to say "I AM THAT I AM" is God Himself. Everyone else is subject to adjustments. In reference to those who are truly His children, He promises to chasten and rebuke those He loves (see Revelation 3:19).

So what's the big deal? Why does God have to be such a cosmic killjoy? Because He knows the consequences of our actions. Because He doesn't really relish the idea of His creations "receiving in themselves that recompence of their error which was meet" (Romans 1:27 KJV). Or, as another translation puts it, "as a result, [those who continually practice sin without repentance] suffered within themselves the penalty they so richly deserved. When they refused to acknowledge God, he abandoned them to their evil minds and let them do things that should never be done. Their lives became full of every kind of wickedness..." (verses 27-28 NLT). And that is exactly where Satan wants us. This gives him an entrée to sear the conscience. Once this occurs, those who have fallen for this deception find themselves lost in the maze of justifying their sin, never coming to the realization they have now allowed their sin to come between themselves and God. And the consequences of their errors can now wreak havoc in their lives unchecked.

Wickedness and Disobedience—whether they enter someone's life through ignorance or deliberate rebellion—

eventually send invitations to Satan and his cohorts to ransack a life. Oh, they might not move in right away. They're
perfectly happy to wait around for a while, then make their
move when their presence will be truly devastating.

Remember, Satan is the accuser of the brethren. You better
believe that the minute you look as if you're *thinking* about
considering disobedience, he's knocking on heaven's door,
bopping into the throne room, and pointing a finger in your
direction, saying, "There he is! He did it! I've now been given
the go-ahead to curse his life. Now, I know that You love him
and all, but if I'm reading my Bible correctly, it says that if he
does this, he'll suffer from that. He's on my turf now because
I know You can't lie. So don't even think about protecting
him! Oh, by the way, Sally Sue didn't pay her tithe last week
so I get to run a number on her finances. And You don't have
the right to rebuke me on her behalf, either! Oooh, I just love
this! Oh, well, You wrote the book, baby. Peace, I'm out!"

Yes, the devil does know his scriptural rights. Do you
know yours? Remember: "the curse causeless shall not come"
(Proverbs 26:2 KJV). The devil cannot curse your life if you
choose actions that lead to blessings. It's up to you. Don't
give the devil an invitation to ransack your life.

Satan loves how we misconstrue those chapters in
Deuteronomy that encourage us to choose life over death
and blessings over curses by being obedient to the Word of
God. Though blessings by grace do exist, God also gives us
what are called conditional blessings. The redemptive work
of Jesus on the cross is sadly misinterpreted by many Christians today as something that canceled out the Old Testament
and its laws, but this is not the case. Jesus came "that the righteousness of the law might be fulfilled in us, who walk not
after the flesh, but after the Spirit" (Romans 8:4 KJV). As we
believe in Him, we are empowered to be obedient to God—
not for justification but in order to live victorious lives—in

order to keep us legally out of Satan's reach. The law was given to us for our own protection.

Laying Down the Law

So what is the purpose of the law? The law was meant to give us knowledge of what God considered sin. This has not changed, folks. God still doesn't think it's a good idea to have other gods, fornicate, commit adultery, steal, kill...you know the laundry list. No way can we ignore what God had to say in the Old Testament. Yes, salvation is free, Jesus became a curse for us, and all that good stuff. But if we want to reach back into the sin box, we then open the door for all those curses to move right back into our lives and set up shop. And Satan will rightfully point out that we invited him. God cannot go against His own word. Therefore, if you choose to violate His word, He has no choice but to allow you to suffer the consequences, which Satan will be more than happy to dole out.

Paul says in Romans 3:31, "Well then, if we emphasize faith, does this mean that we can forget about the law? Of course not! In fact, only when we have faith do we truly fulfill the law" (NLT). Furthermore, Paul says, "So since God's grace has set us free from the law, does this mean we can go on sinning? Of course not! Don't you realize that whatever you choose to obey becomes your master? You can choose sin, which leads to death, or you can choose to obey God and receive his approval" (Romans 6:15-16 NLT). In other words, once you extend your hand to sin you are no longer running things. Sin has you; you don't have sin. Ask any crack addict who's really running their world.

James 1:25 says, "If you keep looking steadily into God's perfect law—the law that sets you free—and if you do what it says and don't forget what you heard, then God will bless you for doing it" (NLT). And here's another passage: "Those who sin are opposed to the law of God, for all sin opposes the law of God. And you know that Jesus came to take away our sins, for there is no sin in him. So if we continue to live in him, we won't sin either. But those who keep on sinning have never known him or understood who he is" (1 John 3:4-6 NLT).

Now that's a deep statement: "Those who keep on sinning have never known him or understood who he is." To know Him is to love Him, to love Him is to obey Him—pure and simple. Think of any love relationship gone wrong. In most cases, one of the members involved doesn't have a clue as to why the relationship is breaking down. He or she is doing everything possible to make the other person happy, but that person remains displeased. Then in a counseling session, an offense that is perpetually repeated comes to light. One frustrated person turns to the other and says, "I told you I don't like it when you do this, and you just keep doing it over and over again!" Or, "I kept asking you to do this and that for me, and you kept ignoring me. I've had enough!" Usually the other person looks back in complete amazement and says, "I don't understand why that one little thing makes you so upset."

This is the statement of someone who never took the time to truly know and understand their mate. They assumed that if they did *most* of what they thought the other expected, a few irritations wouldn't make a difference one way or the other. But this one little thing has now eroded their relationship to the brink of collapsing. The bottom line in most troubled relationships is that someone is giving their partner what *they* think they *need* instead of what their partner really *wants*.

So if God doesn't really need us to run around performing for Him, what does He really want? I say this repeatedly: God is not as interested in us *doing* as He is in us *being* what He has called us to be. God wants our obedience, and He is not impressed with anything else. Jesus made it very clear what

He desired from those who claim to be in a relationship with Him: "'Not all people who sound religious are really godly. They may refer to me as "Lord," but they still won't enter the Kingdom of Heaven. The decisive issue is whether they obey my Father in heaven. On judgment day many will tell me, "Lord, Lord, we prophesied in your name and cast out demons in your name and performed many miracles in your name." But I will reply, "I never knew you. Go away; the things you did were unauthorized"'" (Matthew 7:21-23 NLT).

In other words, "I didn't ask you to do anything for Me. I don't count you among My friends because you lived your life at enmity with Me. You were disobedient to My Father. Even I was obedient to the Word of My Father, and I am God. What made you think you were exempt? How can you say you love Me or know Me, and then carry on the way you do? I'm not at all convinced you had My interests at heart." And it is perfectly fair for Him to feel that way. After all, how many enemies do you invite into your home? How do you decide who is friend or foe? By considering their intentions and actions toward you. Those who continually offend you are not considered friends.

When people really care or are really in love, they trip over themselves not to offend the object of their affection. They are always seeking to please, seeking to find out more about what the other likes and requires in order to be happy. It becomes a pleasure to serve. No sacrifice is too great for the one who makes their heart go pitty-pat. They are forever collecting data on the object of their affection. If someone came bearing a lie about that person, they would be quick to defend them and say, "I know this person; they wouldn't do that." Yet many commit all sorts of things that are contrary to the Word of God, qualifying them with statements like, "The Lord told me to do this," or, "I felt led to do that." If they really knew the Savior, they would know what they were hearing was the voice of the Deceiver, Temptation, attempting to take advantage of their lack of knowledge of the One they claim to belong to.

"But I thought they were Christians!" is a much-used exclamation from those in the world referring to church people who fail to live up to their expectations of what Christians should be like. Perhaps this is why Jesus said, "Therefore by their fruits you will know them" (Matthew 7:20 NKJV). So many tiptoe around this issue in the name of "not judging folks." But many misunderstand the definition of judging. Judging means deciding the final verdict on a person's case, and that is not our job. By all means, don't judge. God will be the final judge. (After all, He's the only one who knows the whole story on that person.) But by all means, feel free to fruit-inspect. Those who consistently and willfully sin without repentance do not really know Christ. That's not Michelle speaking; that's the Bible.

Living Above the Law

Why does James 1:22 tell us to be "doers of the word, and not hearers only" (KJV)? What is the Word? It is more than the work of Jesus at the cross. It is the heart of God and how He wants His children to live, not only for our own sakes but also for the sake of the world. After taking a recent trip, I have a new appreciation for David's words in Psalm 23:3: "He leads me in paths of righteousness for *His name's sake*" (NKJV, emphasis added).

Some time back I was traveling with a group of performers who were mostly Christians. However, there were a few unsaved people in the group. During the trip, several of the Christians began doing things that were definitely questionable to the unsaved members of the cast. They reacted with overwhelming disgust and disappointment, saying that they were better "Christians" than those who claimed to be.

This became their justification for continuing on in their unsaved spiritual state. I was very saddened by this because I could not defend my other cast mates' behavior. Their actions were wrong and ungodly, and an opportunity to witness had been ruined. I could only be responsible for walking in a solid manner before them myself and hope it would make a difference.

Perhaps we should revisit the meaning of the word *Christian*. It means "follower of Christ." It is an action word, not a description of a belief. In most cases, Christians are the only Bible the world reads. If we're slippin', dippin', and livin' the way the rest of the world does, we assist them in justifying their state of spiritual decay. They feel that they are better Christians than we are, so what do they need Jesus for? Think about it. You, in the midst of your sin, might be holding up someone else's salvation. God will hold you accountable for that lost soul.

Let me give a sobering fact to those of you who want to keep living the way you've been living in hopes that God knows where you live and understands your weaknesses: God understands, but Satan does not. Satan is not in the mood to be sensitive and understanding. He is out for blood. Some who live in blatant sin while waving the banner of Christianity have deceived themselves because they continue to prosper and do just fine. I have one word for this type of saint: Careful! The devil will bless you to bind you. And when he's sure he's got you good and secure, he will strike a lethal blow that will cost you all you've acquired. Samson, too, was deceived when he continued to win battles against the Philistines. But there came a day when the umbrella of grace grew too tattered to keep covering him, and his end was tragic.

I hate to sound like Mr. Rogers, but the law is our friend, boys and girls. It gives us wholesome boundaries to enjoy the liberty that God gives us through His Son. We are now free to live above sin and death. "Therefore if the Son makes you free, you shall be free indeed" (John 8:36 NKJV). Will you attempt to make God a liar? As a new Christian, whenever I found myself staring Temptation in the face, I would remind my soul, "What shall we say then? Shall we continue in sin, that grace may abound? God forbid. How shall we, that are dead to sin, live any longer therein?" (Romans 6:1-2 KJV). Another translation says, "Shall we sin to our heart's content and see how far we can exploit the grace of God?...We have died, once and for all to sin; can we breathe its air again?"[2]

How to Avoid a Heart Attack

Now that I've opened up a whole can of worms by advocating that we not ignore the law, I want to make it perfectly clear that this in no way is an invitation for anyone to "become religious." Memorizing and obeying the law by rote is not the answer. For one thing, no one can keep up this exercise. The law becomes perfected in us when it is engrafted on our hearts because of our love for Christ. This is a little secret that Temptation knows well. This is why he encourages you to be suspicious of God's motives toward you. This is why he encourages you to become angry and bitter toward God. Temptation has planned a devious strategy to attack your heart. He knows that your heart toward God will determine your obedience to Him. Remember this? "If you love Me, keep My commandments" (John 14:15 NKJV). That's all God asks from you as proof of your love. Human beings ask for that and much more.

Don't miss this, because it's important! A church mentioned in the book of Revelation did and said all the right things, but God accused them of forsaking their first love— Him. You can read about this church in Revelation 2:1-7. They had "gotten religious." They didn't love God as they did at first—or love each other, for that matter. Have you ever met some Christians who were just downright mean and ornery or depressed and murmuring continually? They were busy working at the church all the time—they'd even show up with cookies for the sick—but they were just plain unpleasant to be around. They had grown bitter from going through the motions of Christianity. Gone was the passion that is present when you're in love.

We must be ever mindful that obedience and everything else that goes with this Christian walk should be borne out of a love relationship with Jesus. If you must be a slave, be a love slave. It's far more enjoyable! If I had a choice of being bound to a thing, a compulsion, or a good relationship, I would take the relationship. Relationship, relationship, relationship...I can't say that word enough. God is bored with religion, and we should be, too. There is no joy in it. You know why? Religion is a tool that Satan designed for bondage. Now not only do you have to follow God's rules, you also have to follow a bunch of rules that some men you don't even know made up! It's enough to make you get so disgusted that you want to chuck the whole thing out the window. We humans are such extremists. A man of God offends us, so we get rid of God, too. How about throwing out the bath water and keeping the baby? It's not the baby's fault that the water is dirty. As we pass through life, dirt will land on us. How long we let it stay there is up to us.

But Satan works overtime on our hearts. He knows if he can get the heart sewn up, his work is finished. And that actually brings us full circle, doesn't it? When we're in love, really in love, we become consumed with figuring out how to please the object of our affections. But when we become disgruntled with that person, we close up shop and take our toys and our heart home. Love is the basis of all worship. You're going to hear that word a lot—*worship*. Satan is after the heart because it is the seat of worship. And Satan knows that people in love experience feelings of insecurity from time to time. *Is he really going to keep his promise? Does he really love me? Will he still love me if I do this?* Satan loves to make us ask those questions.

Of course God still loves us when we sin. After all, we're the ones who really suffer. We merely grieve the Holy Spirit, but we hurt ourselves: "Do not be deceived, God is not mocked; for whatever a man sows, that he will also reap" (Galatians 6:7 NKJV). Satan knows that, so why don't you believe it? But we prefer to listen to the serpent's reassurance, "Ye shall not surely die" (Genesis 3:4 KJV). What a liar! A woman dies a little inside every time she lies with a man and then gets rejected. A drug addict dies a little with every puff, every sniff, every prick of the needle. A businessman dies a little inside every time he makes a dishonest deal. On and on the cycle of life goes, with people committing suicide by the millimeter every time they're not true to existing the way God designed them to.

And for those who take the easy way out by simply not taking a stand one way or another, the price tag in the end is just as high: Evil flourishes when good men do nothing. Allowing ungodly practices to continue uninterrupted bears its own consequences. God holds us accountable as watchmen on the walls of our churches, our communities, our nations. This cancels out Satan's counsel to shut up and tolerate the sin of those in our midst. You can call it "minding your own business" if you want to, but depending on the situation, compromise can fall under the heading "sin of omission." This breaks down into two areas—not answering to what God has called us to do, and not holding others accountable to what God's Word says. Sometimes by doing and saying nothing, we get into more trouble than if we'd just thrown caution to the wind, been obedient, and trusted

God to work out the best results. Leave important information off of your next tax return, get caught by the IRS, and see what happens. The same applies in the spiritual realm.

Don't believe me? Then believe the voice of the Lord:

> If I warn the wicked, saying, "You are under the penalty of death," but you fail to deliver the warning, they will die in their sins. And I will hold you responsible, demanding your blood for theirs. If you warn them and they keep on sinning and refuse to repent, they will die in their sins. But you will have saved your life because you did what you were told to do. If good people turn bad and don't listen to my warning, they will die. If you did not warn them of the consequences, then they will die in their sins. Their previous good deeds won't help them, and I will hold you responsible, demanding your blood for theirs. But if you warn them and they repent, they will live, and you will have saved your own life, too (Ezekiel 3:18-21 NLT).

For all you lovers of the New Testament, try this one on for size: "Take no part in the worthless deeds of evil and darkness; instead, rebuke and expose them" (Ephesians 5:11 NLT). Or how about this one:

> You are not to associate with anyone who claims to be a Christian yet indulges in sexual sin, or is greedy, or worships idols, or is abusive, or a drunkard, or a swindler. Don't even eat with such people. It isn't [your] responsibility to judge outsiders [those who are not Christians], but it certainly is your job to judge those inside the church who are sinning in these ways. God will judge those on the outside; but as the Scriptures say, "You must remove the evil person from among you" (1 Corinthians 5:11-13 NLT).

This came after Paul encouraged members of the Corinthian church to expel a man who was living in sin with his father's wife. He instructed them to "call a meeting of the church....Then you must cast this man out of the church and into Satan's hands, so that his sinful nature will be destroyed and he himself will be saved when the Lord returns" (1 Corinthians 5:4-5 NLT).

Strong words with heavy connotations! Words like these make the church of today very uncomfortable, so in many cases these Scriptures are not spoken of. And the church is going to hell in a handbasket because of the manipulations of the Prince of Darkness, who encourages us to keep our sin, and the sins of others, under wraps and silently hope for the best. Yet the Bible tells us to expect the worst if we continue in this light—pardon the pun.

Ignorance, the Silent Killer

Sometimes I wonder if Samson's life would have been any different if his parents had just put their foot down and refused to go along with his marriage to a Philistine woman. Would it have thwarted the downward spiral of his life? Would it have saved Israel from some of the troubles they experienced because of his folly? Or what of Achan, and what his sin did to an entire camp in the seventh chapter of Joshua? The cover-up of his sin resulted in the loss of a number of innocent lives. Or what of Aaron, the brother of Moses? His simple omission to take a stand when the Israelites cried out for an idol to worship caused devastation in the camp. It is important to realize that everything we do (or don't do, in some cases) affects everybody, everywhere, all the time. In the end, sin is like cigar smoke. It gets in the hair and clothing of everyone who happens to be nearby. Sometimes I wonder if we don't realize how our own personal stumbles affect so many others. God is the first to sadly say, "My people are destroyed for lack of knowledge" (Hosea 4:6 KJV).

Surely all sin is not deliberate. If a sinful act is not done on purpose, it is generally done out of ignorance, which is really the design of Deception. Actually, even that which is done on purpose is rooted in deception. Praise God that He is able to redeem all things. Though we shouldn't rest on our laurels and purposely track mud through the blood of Jesus, it is good to know that "in all things God works for the good of those who love him, who have been called according to his purpose" (Romans 8:28 NIV). Though this verse speaks to a specific audience, what it really tells us is that God is ultimately in control of everything that takes place in our lives. In His omniscience, He already knows every slip, every dip, and every splash we will make into the pool of sin. He has gone before us with an insurance plan to salvage our lives after we've made our mistakes. "To him belong strength and victory; both deceived and deceiver are his" (Job 12:16 NIV).

Whether he likes it or not, Satan is merely a pawn—even in the midst of his own cruel game. God allows him to mess with us and test us in order to teach us valuable lessons. So if that's the case, why do we still need to master our own flesh and overcome Temptation? Let me put it to you in the form of a question. Which would you prefer—a car that had been pieced together with materials collected from a junkyard, or a shiny, brand-new car that had never been in an accident or sideswiped or damaged in any way? If you've got the money, a car can be repaired, no matter how bad the damage. But the bottom line is, it never quite runs the same. How you decide to finish your journey is up to you.

2

TO MASTER OR
BE MASTERED

"Sin is crouching at your door; it desires to have you,
but you must master it."

GENESIS 4:7 NIV

W HAT MAKES TEMPTATION SUCH A CRAFTY genius at catching
others in its sticky web? Temptation knows exactly where to
strike—the heart of man, that soft, pliable place within us all
called *self*. The place that screams for attention, with no
thought of the consequences. For those who do stop momen-
tarily to consider the cost of giving in to temptation, the ratio-
nalization arises that there must be some way to get what
they want without hurting anyone else. But! Sometimes
things happen. Others do get hurt as we grab for the ring.
Self placates the grabber by assuring him, "Hey, that's life! It's
every man for himself—bottom line." This is the selfish voice
that cried out from Cain, "Am I my brother's keeper?" (Genesis 4:9 NIV). Translated into modern-day vernacular, he was
saying, "Hey, sounds a like a personal problem to me. I can't

worry about anyone else; I've got to cover my own back. If I don't take care of me, no one else will." But sin is never that simple. The innocent blood of Cain's brother, Abel, cried out from the ground. The problem Cain thought he had gotten rid of when he bid Abel good riddance turned into a greater liability. His life was cursed and, ironically, his only source of salvation was God's covering, which he had initially despised.

Contrary to popular belief, no matter how independent you fancy yourself, in the immortal words of Bob Dylan, "You gotta serve somebody." However, you do have a choice of either serving sin, which leads to bondage, or the One who leads us to liberation.

In Romans chapter 6, Paul says, "We should no longer be slaves to sin—because anyone who has died has been freed from sin" (verses 6-7 NIV). Paul urges us not to "let sin reign in your mortal body so that you obey its evil desires" (verse 12 NIV). He goes on to tell us that "you are slaves to the one whom you obey—whether you are slaves to sin, which leads to death, or to obedience, which leads to righteousness" (verse 16 NIV). He exhorts us, "Just as you used to offer the parts of your body in slavery to impurity and to ever-increasing wickedness, so now offer them in slavery to righteousness leading to holiness" (verse 19 NIV). His dissertation ends on a note of encouragement and hope by offering this perspective: "When you were slaves to sin, you were free from the control of righteousness....But now that you have been set free from sin and have become slaves to God, the benefit you reap leads to holiness, and the result is eternal life" (verses 20,22 NIV).

I think that if I had a choice between those two masters, I would choose God. How about you? I would choose being a love slave any day over being a slave performing hard labor with no reward but eternal damnation for my services. Satan is a cruel taskmaster operating a sweatshop business with no insurance, no retirement plan, no workers' compensation, and no severance pay. All you get from him are paychecks that bounce. Though the checks initially look good, the end result, once they've been cashed, is always feelings of emptiness, hopelessness, and despair.

So why do we fall for Satan's same old lines time and time again? Because the morsels of sin that he waves under our noses look so, well, tempting! Like the manufacturer of a brand-new credit card with unlimited credit, Satan urges us to let ourselves go and have a good time because, after all, we deserve it. But sooner or later the credit card bill arrives and we find ourselves bankrupt. Some of us who find ourselves in this position are nearly pushed over the brink. The only way out is suicide—spiritually, physically, financially, or reputationally. Let's face it, Romans 6:23 gives us the bottom line. The wages of sin always was, and always will be, death.

God, on the other hand, promises that His yoke is easy and His burden is light. He has an incredible insurance plan: "Though he fall, [the righteous] shall not be utterly cast down; for the LORD upholds him with His hand. I have been young, and now am old; yet I have not seen the righteous forsaken, nor his descendants begging bread. He is ever merciful, and lends; and his descendants are blessed" (Psalm 37:24 NKJV). Talk about being in good hands. Look out, Allstate! His retirement plan sounds better than moving to Florida: "You will show me the path of life; in Your presence is fullness of joy; at Your right hand are pleasures forevermore" (Psalm 16:11 NKJV). And can we discuss workers' comp? "There remaineth therefore a rest to the people of God" (Hebrews 4:9 KJV). God's severance plan isn't shabby, either: "To live is Christ and to die is gain" (Philippians 1:21 NIV). Stack that up next to the stock exchange! I would definitely want to work for a company that offered a package like that. And God, always being just and fair, leaves the choice completely up to you. The end benefits of life or death, blessings or curses, are connected to whom you serve.

Master of Your Own Ship

Temptation's first strategy is to make us rationalize that the requests of our flesh are reasonable because we are entitled to them. After all, we deserve to have what we want, right? This is the reasoning that opens the door to entrapment more often than not. In the film *Fatal Attraction,* viewers were mortified to watch what one man assumed would be a harmless and pleasurable one-night stand turn into a nightmare that threatened the well-being of his family, his career, his reputation, and, finally, his very life.

Like the heroes of Greek mythology, who were lured by the Sirens' beauty and enticing songs only to find themselves caught in a state of madness, enslavement, or destruction, many Christians find their lives shipwrecked after indulging in what they imagined to be a harmless dalliance. Entitlement is a serious deceiver. Satan thought he was entitled to the praises he had been gathering for God the Almighty. This reasoning led him to high treason in the heavenlies. How Satan managed to convince one-third of the heavenly beings that he was the man of the hour to follow is not revealed in Scripture, but I could write a screenplay loaded with suppositions.

Every kingdom has two common groups of subjects—the content and the disgruntled. I think it's safe to say that Satan appealed to the disgruntled group. I can picture him now, quite literally promising them the world, if they would follow only him. I can hear him saying, "Exactly who does God think He is, anyway? Why should He get all the praise while we do all the work? I think it's high time we get our just due." And with that proclamation, a rallying cry went up from the disgruntled crowd, which gave the devil all the ammunition he needed to go forth and conquer.

But Satan overlooked a major fact in his mad dash for the throne. He had completely underestimated God while over-estimating his own power. He forgot he was a created being, totally dependent—whether he cared to admit it or not—on his Creator. And so Satan's dance with rebellion landed him in the exact spot he was trying to avoid. To his horror, he found himself standing on the sidelines of kingdom living along with his cronies, banned from the dance floor while others he considered beneath himself—namely, humans—enjoyed the waltz of righteousness, peace, and fulfillment in the Holy Ghost as they danced joyfully to God's tune. A seething wallflower, Satan paced the fringes of the festivities, devising a way to ruin the ball. After all, how dare anyone else have a good time while he was feeling miserable? Not one to admit defeat, he decided there was more than one way to accomplish his mission of acquiring God-status. If he had been able to influence one-third of the heavenly beings, why couldn't he influence these mere mortals?

How to go about luring these humans away from the fes-tivities became an intriguing question to Satan. *Aha!* Perhaps he could use his own mistake to seduce them off the dance floor. He realized that they, too, would like the idea of being in control of their own lives. Who in their right mind would choose to be subservient, anyway? He would very subtly plant this whole "lord of your own destiny" seed in their hearts and watch what happened. Never mind that they had been created to discern evil rather than experience it. He would fix that! A hint here, a little mood music there, and they would go for the carrot—or, rather, the apple—before they knew what hit them. Of course, they didn't need to know *all* the details. The reality that they could never be independent agents was insignificant, and certainly to Satan's advantage if he kept them in the dark.

Now, how should Satan go about this delicate operation? He couldn't trust any of his demon followers. This assignment was far too important. Let's see, humans liked pretty things. Hmm...after some thought, he decided that the serpent would be his mode of entry. After all, the animal was downright hypnotic. Certainly it was the most subtle of all the creatures God had made (see Genesis 3:1), and it definitely had a way with words. Satan had already perceived that questions were always more effective than statements. Questions could always lead to weeds of discontentment and curiosity. And both of these weeds had the capacity to grow at such a rapid rate that they would mar the beauty of any garden in no time flat. So the snake waited for a rest in the music before uttering the famous question: "Did God really say, 'You must not eat from any tree in the garden'?" (Genesis 3:1 NIV). And the rest of the story is history.

Truth or Consequences

From the beginning of time, those who have found themselves having a conversation with the devil have netted the same results, with the exception of Jesus. After all, Satan makes everything sound so reasonable, even if his proposition is highly improbable. Do you really believe that Eve thought she could ever reach the status of being like God? No! The Bible says, "When the woman saw that the tree was good for food, and that it was pleasant to the eyes, and a tree to be desired to make one wise, she took of the fruit thereof, and did eat." And then, because we always like to have a partner in crime, she "gave also unto her husband with her; and he did eat" (Genesis 3:6 KJV). Imagine that! Peer pressure began with one person. Never underestimate the ability of one person to influence someone else to go against his or her better judgment. For the Bible makes it plain that "Adam was not deceived, but the woman being deceived was in the transgression" (1 Timothy 2:14 KJV).

Adam made an intelligent decision to partake in what could be considered blatant disobedience. For Adam, more was at stake than tasting a piece of fruit. He had to keep peace between himself and Eve at all costs. He had just started really getting into this marriage thing, and he liked it! I believe that, in Adam's mind, he thought that if there were any negative consequences resulting from this action, he would be able to reason with God. After all, in Adam's mind, the fault would be attributed to the Creator because He was the one who had given him the woman. But we'll discuss self-justification in a later chapter.

Anyway, the serpent was cute, the fruit looked tasty, and Adam had dismissed thoughts of any impending conse-quences from his mind. Hey, what harm could a little bite of fruit do? And surely God wouldn't be opposed to Adam and Eve gaining a little wisdom. He couldn't possibly be that unreasonable, could He?

Unfortunately, from Adam and Eve's time right up to today, the story's ending is always painfully predictable—horror at the unanticipated consequences. Take, for example, that last-minute fling before the wedding that means nothing until several years later when a doctor solemnly delivers the verdict of HIV-positive to a shocked couple. An entire family is affected, and all the tears and regret in the world will not erase the consequences of a dance with the devil. And so it was with Adam and Eve. Their family—that includes you and me and the entire world—was affected by their decision to disobey God in a moment of experimentation. Sin began a race with righteousness to see which would be the strongest family trait to be passed down through the generations. Thankfully, the marathon is almost over.

This Is a Test

We all have grown used to the periodic appearance of color bars on our television screens that are accompanied by a high-pitched, piercing sound. Then we hear the comforting voice of an announcer assuring us, "This has been a test of the Emergency Broadcasting System. Should this have been an actual emergency, you would be informed as to where to tune for further instructions. Again, this is only a test." If only life were so simple!

In order to master temptation, the first thing we must understand is that temptation is merely a test. Temptation is Satan testing your allegiance to God. Jesus said, "If you love Me, keep My commandments" (John 14:15 NKJV). Entitlement screams, "I love *me* more! I love what *I* want more! Therefore, I deserve to have what I *want!* Forget *You,* God. You have everything, so why can't I have this one little thing?" In order to answer that question, we must be able to understand the heart of God.

Like a loving parent warning a naïve toddler not to touch the hot stove, God gently warns us not to venture within harm's reach. But, being as curious as children, we run smiling toward the flame, thinking, *Surely He jests,* or *It couldn't be that serious,* or even more foolishly, *It won't burn me.* But we find that it does. And so, with tears streaming down our faces, clutching stinging fingers, we run back to Him to make it all better. Unfortunately, while He can wipe away our tears with His forgiveness, He is unable to erase the consequences, which stem from a law that is separate from His love. This is what He knew all along, but either we didn't ask, couldn't wait for an explanation, or, worse yet, refused to trust His judgment.

I remember that, as a child, whenever I asked my father why I couldn't do something, his reply remained the same in every instance: "Because I said so." How I hated those words!

Nothing could speed up my heart's rhythm like those words! *How dare he not give me an explanation? Who does he think he is?* my little inexperienced mind would scream. But the real problem was that I didn't think about who *he* was. He was my father who loved me, and he felt responsible for protecting me. He had been where I thought I wanted to go. He already knew what was waiting at the end of that road, and he wanted me to avoid the pitfalls. Also, he understood that it was important for me to learn obedience for the sake of obedience and the respect of authority for my own welfare as I walked through life.

The world doesn't always offer explanations, yet we sometimes are more willing to take the commands of mere men over God, whose intentions toward us are always pure. "For I know the thoughts that I think toward you, saith the LORD, thoughts of peace, and not of evil, to give you an expected end" (Jeremiah 29:11 KJV). There you have it in a nutshell! God sees the end of the situation. He sees what you are not expecting and what you should avoid. And it is His preference to steer you toward the blessing.

A popular singer stated in a song that the forbidden always added more intrigue to the temptation. Believe me, Satan knows which buttons to push! From the time we begin to crawl, we begin to defy that word that our ears hear countless times throughout the day...*No!* I believe the first three words in every infant's vocabulary are, in respective order, Dada, Mama, and no. Our spirit teaches us to call for our Father, both heavenly and natural, first. Then for Mama, the one who comes to soothe our every cry. And then we begin to utter the word that our parents both begin to say the most as we start to discover the world around us with all of its intriguing delights. You know the ones I'm talking about— electrical outlets, hot stoves, fragile collectibles on glass tabletops, and those wonderful bottles under the sink. These things beckon us to insert a finger or touch or bang or taste, much to the alarm of observing adults.

The tension mounts between child and parent as the command "No!" is shouted and a raised hand of warning is suspended in midair. Ever so tentatively, while keeping an eye on the source of the command, a little hand reaches toward the object it has been warned not to touch. "No!" The word is repeated a little higher in pitch, a little louder. Still the hand inches toward its prize. Now it's a serious standoff. This is the moment that will reveal who is really running the show at this address. "I said no!" Authority makes the first move, fearing the small hand is getting too close for comfort. And when disobedience realizes that it is about to be overpowered by a force much larger than itself, one of two reactions occurs. The first response is a dramatic flinging of the disobedient one's body to the floor to scream and cry in utter frustration at not having his way. The second move is to totter off as quickly as he can on legs that haven't quite solidified their running skills, giggling as if amused by his ability to escape, but only after really working that grown-up's nerves. Children will certainly try you as Satan tries us and as we try God.

Waking Up to Reality

As we grow older, the game is no longer amusing, and the consequences become much more painful. And in case you haven't figured it out by now, temptation is the servant of death. There is no escaping the truth that "each one is tempted when, by his own evil desire, he is dragged away and enticed. Then, after desire has conceived, it gives birth to sin; and sin, when it is full-grown, gives birth to death" (James 1:14-15 NIV).

This is about what a grown-up self, in full knowledge of the twists and turns of the game, chooses to do in the face of what is written. Contrary to our earthly parents, God will not stand with an upraised hand and have a Wild, Wild West standoff with us to see who has the quickest draw. This is not a contest. This is not a showdown. Yet it *is* a matter of life and death. God has given us His written Word and the counseling of the Holy Spirit to guide us. The rest is up to us. God is a gentleman. He will not force His will on anyone. After all, we are adults. We should know better.

And in that knowing there is no more room for excuses. No longer can we cry, "It was the woman You gave me! It was the man You gave me! It was the father, or the mother, You gave me! It was the situation You allowed!" The Bible tells us it is our own evil desires that pull us away from God when we are beckoned by temptation. That reality flies in the face of the world's present-day philosophy that encourages us to find someone—anyone—to blame instead of ourselves. The world tells us that we must be the victim of someone or something else. We would never dream of doing wrong things just on the basis of self-compulsion. Yet God answers back, "It was your own desire!"

Let's face it. If you've never smoked a cigarette, the confident Marlboro man smiling down at you from a billboard or an ad picturing the coolest Camel in the world are not going to make you start searching in ashtrays for a cigarette stub. But if you've smoked in the past and have now quit, these tantalizing reminders hold the potential to set you back and cause you to backslide, even if you rationalize that it's for just one last puff. As you can see, Opportunity does not perform well alone on the stage of temptation. It needs to sing a duet with Desire. Opportunity without the presence of Desire sings to an uninterested audience. Desire without Opportunity only entertains the frustrated. But when Opportunity and Desire tune up together…well, now you've got a sinful act *and* a captive audience!

So, who are the players in this drama? How will the plot unfold? Will the villain finally capture his prey? And is the unsuspecting victim as unsuspecting as we think? All these questions and more will be explored as we unravel "the lion's tail" (the devil's *modus operandi*), so to speak.

3

THE WORLD, THE FLESH, AND THE DEVIL

"For all that is in the world—the lust of the flesh, the lust of the eyes, and the pride of life—is not of the Father but is of the world."

1 JOHN 2:16 NKJV

YEARS AGO, A FAMOUS COMEDIAN'S favorite punch line was, "Honey, the devil made me do it." Meanwhile, an incredible singing group crooned, "That's the way of the world." And research shows that when it comes to earning big money at the box office, "flesh sells."

So what is really the ticket that draws? Certainly it takes a well-thought-out set of tactics to close the sale, no matter how appealing the offer. Most intelligent buyers like to know the cost first, and then check their budget. Perhaps this is why many stores make the price tags on their merchandise so difficult to find. Their strategy is to get you to instantly fall in love with the item with the hope that this will compel you to throw all reason to the wind and make an impulse purchase. In most cases, victims of this ploy later experience what is called buyer's remorse. However, by then they are either too embarrassed or too weary of the whole ordeal to make the additional effort to return the item.

It works almost every time, and that's because all of these seemingly covert manipulations were mulled over and worked out long before you stepped through the entrance. The lighting, the music, the atmosphere, the advertisements—they're all designed to make you spend what, in most cases, you don't have. I spent years working as a copywriter and art director in the advertising world, crafting commercials to make the masses salivate. Sometimes I almost felt guilty as I wrote copy designed to seduce someone to drop everything they were doing to fulfill their Big Mac attack or created a scene to make every viewer thirsty for a Coca Cola. But creating those ads was my job, and I did it with relish, embracing each new challenge to make a specific product desirable. If only people knew how much sweat and agony go into creating a thirty-second television commercial! The research, the meetings, the discussions, the planning, the hours spent laboring are not to be believed. With all of this advertising experience under my belt, I have a pretty good idea of how Satan has set up his devious marketing strategy to appeal to the masses.

Satanic Marketing 101

Allow me to set up a mock scenario to illustrate how Satan's kingdom would run if he were in the advertising business. The setting is the dark side's creative conference room. Lucifer himself, the reigning creative director, is overseeing the meeting. As the man in charge, his role is to hand out assignments and approve or disapprove of the campaigns that are presented to him by his employees. He has the final say on whether each campaign is capable of moving his hot new product—Sin Perfume. His mission is for the world to smell of this fragrance to high heaven.

And so the various teams, looking a little harried, gather to make their presentations to the head honcho. They've done their homework, but Lucifer is a harsh taskmaster! It seems that he's never satisfied.

"Sometimes I think he expects nothing short of a miracle from us," one employee says when out of his boss's earshot.

"Well, that's not our department," comes the frustrated reply from another worker while all the others nod their heads in agreement. And so, filing into the conference room, their findings in hand, they make ready for yet another lengthy and intense meeting.

Breathing a sigh of relief, the strategic planning team settles back in their chairs as members of the research group take their places. The researchers have a difficult job. They have to be familiar with everything there is to know about the target market. This massive assignment requires a lot of leg-work and long hours of tedious observance. Still, their findings are generally interesting and very useful in helping them prepare marketing strategies. However, they aren't always able to master the art of anticipating shifts in the market. Sometimes they've been accused of complacency when it seems that, once they get used to the habits of their subjects, they tend to relax on the job. The researchers, in turn, blame their lack of competency on the prayers of the saints, which cause confusion among Lucifer's staff. But that excuse is always lost on the ears of their easily riled boss, who then turns to rail accusations of failure on the rest of the departments for not being efficient in their respective functions. After all, everyone knows the ultimate rule is to prevent prayer at all costs.

"So what do we have today? Make it snappy. We haven't got eternity, you know. Time is of the essence!" Lucifer barks

On that note, the meeting commences with the head of research pacing nervously as he reports his latest findings. "Well...uh...it...er...seems that humans have remained pretty consistent down through the ages. They are still drawn to things that are pleasing to the eye or appeal to their lower, fleshly nature or promote their ego."

"So tell us something we don't know!" Lucifer interjects.

"Yes, sir. I was just trying to give a little background..."

"Well, skip the background and get on with it!"

"Yes, sir," continues the head of research. "As I was saying, we already know that the worldly populace at large have been faithful consumers of Sin Perfume. But the discovery which we find exciting is that, contrary to popular belief, Christians are just as viable a market to tap into!"

An excited hum begins to generate around the conference room as others start to shuffle their notes, frantically reaching for pens and notepads as they whisper to their colleagues. "Silence!" Lucifer glares around the room, and conversation screeches to an abrupt halt. He leans forward in his chair, obviously interested. "I'm listening...continue."

"It seems that even Christians have a dark side, so to speak. Even though they are a sensitive market, they can be convinced to buy our brand. It's simply a matter of capturing their attention at the right time, in the right place, while they are in the right frame of mind. You know, kinda like what we did with Adam and Eve."

Again a buzz begins around the room, but a glance from the head of the table silences the noise.

"Isolation is crucial with this market. Personal fulfillment works as effective, attractive packaging, and the promise of making consumers feel good gets their attention, especially if the item seems exclusive and slightly out of their reach," the head of research says. "And last, but certainly not least, we need to appeal to their longing for independence. Even the most sanctimonious Christian battles with that."

"Well, who wouldn't get tired of wearing a fragrance called Eau de Holiness, anyway?" a member of the creative team snickers.

"And whose crazy idea was it to make their fragrance an oil? Our spray is so much nicer," reasoned another.

"And who came up with that awful cross on that blood-red background for a logo?" wondered one of the art directors.

"I know it's considered a costly perfume, but I just don't get how it ever became so popular. And how they could ever say it smells like Joy is beyond me!" says a copywriter.

On that note, the conference room explodes in conversation. "May I *please* finish my presentation?" an exasperated cry cuts through the commotion. The head of research clears his throat and continues. "It is important to note that Christians are fickle consumers. They must be monitored closely, because at any given time they are given to repentance and will revert back to their former brand of fragrance."

"Well, isn't that comforting," Lucifer sneers in disgust. Shifting his gaze, he spots his next nervous presenter. "Well, what can the strategic planning team add to make some sense out of this?"

"Well, sir," the head of strategic planning replies, "if you would allow me to make my presentation on slides, I'm sure you will agree with our approach."

"Fine, I prefer the dark anyway. Someone get the lights and turn on the projector," Lucifer commands.

Feeling as though he has gotten off to a good start, the strategic planning head dives into his discourse. "Since we have pretty much gotten the general worldly populace under our influence, I suggest we concentrate our primary efforts on the Christian market, which should be divided up into several segments. The first segment is children from birth to age seven, especially those who are abused, come from broken homes, or are latchkey children. This segment is wide open. If we gain a stronghold on youth in this age group, there's a good chance we will have them for life, as we'll get them in their most formative years."

"The next target group," he continues, "is young people ages thirteen through twenty-one. At this age, humans are prime for experimentation and usurping authority. Preachers' kids are often easy targets, as are the fatherless. And our next prime segment is females ages fourteen to forty. Their search for love and success to validate their identities makes them willing to sample almost anything they think will help them accomplish their goals."

The strategic planning head grows more excited as he prepares to announce his final disclosure. "The last segment is our most important—males fourteen to forty. The earlier we capture this group, the better. This will prevent them from rising up to be strong spiritual leaders in their homes and communities. Why, if we are successful in gaining their business, our profit margin will soar!"

The din in the room becomes deafening as another member of the strategic planning team scuttles forward and deposits one last slide into the speaker's hand.

"Ah, yes, one final segment. Smaller, but still significant." He pauses for effect. "Those who are weary in well-doing. The dissatisfied and the prideful are always easy targets, as you all should know."

"You've done your work well," Lucifer admits. Yet, not willing to lose his edge, he snaps back to his former disposition. "Account team, what do you have to add?"

"Lights, please!" the account supervisor says. "Per the findings of the research and strategic planning departments, it is our suggestion that the following strategy be utilized. It is our recommendation that the tone of the advertising should be seductive, provocative, and nonthreatening—similar to those sexy perfume commercials. Our brand should broaden its base and develop a full line of products in order to support the main product, Sin Perfume, and appeal to the different segments of the market."

The account supervisor draws in a deep breath. "We've already brainstormed on what some of those complementary products should be for testing. Disobedience Bubble Bath, for starters. This will be an easy sell now that the campaign to dismantle child discipline has proven successful. And Rebellion Shampoo. Position it as the 'in' thing for kids, and it will literally grow wings and fly off the shelves! Manipulation Hair Spray should go over big with the women as long as the main selling point is irresistibility. Deceit Toothpaste should do well with high-powered executive types, while Pride Body Splash will be a sure seller with those in the entertainment field. They *always* believe their own press. And let's not forget those men going through midlife crises. Then again, this product should be a top seller across the board. And now for the *pièce de résistance!* A sure way to diminish prayer! A new line of air fresheners—Distraction, Unbelief, Fatigue, Complacency, Jealousy, Unforgiveness, and Resentment!"

A hum of approval rises in the room. "Once a member of the target audience samples one of these products, he will easily make the transition to our main brand, Sin Perfume." The account executive ends his presentation triumphantly amid the sounds of excitement and returns to his seat.

"Well, what are you waiting for?" Lucifer roars. "Get to work!"

With that, the room clears, and the creative department goes into a frenzy of activity, weaving ad campaigns sure to entice and bewitch anyone who makes the mistake of lending them their attention.

Please don't allow my imaginative interpretation of how Satan functions to fool you in the least or cause you not to take him seriously. Always be aware that we have a very real enemy who in no way takes his mission against us lightly. We should not be ignorant of his devices lest he, as Paul says, should gain advantage over us (see 2 Corinthians 2:11). Trust me, if you give him an inch, he'll take as many miles as he can before you come to your senses and stop him.

The Drama Unfolds

So who is the real culprit when we fall into the trap of sin? As we gaze at the stage of life, we see three principal players battling for dominance in this drama. The flesh stands center stage, quivering as it strives to stand its ground, while the world pulls from stage right and the devil pulls from stage left. The words of Paul echo from behind the curtain like a fuzzy memory: "In time past ye walked according to the course of this world, according to the prince of the power of the air, the spirit that now worketh in the children of disobedience: among whom also we all had our conversation in times past in the lusts of our flesh, fulfilling the desires of the flesh and of the mind; and were by nature the children of wrath, even as others" (Ephesians 2:2-4 KJV). We nod our heads in agreement and pray, "God forbid we resume our past conversation!" "But it is my nature! I can't help myself!" the flesh cries out in a dramatic plea for understanding. Again comes the challenging voice: "Those controlled by the sinful nature cannot please God. You, however, are controlled not by the sinful nature but by the Spirit, if the Spirit of God lives in you. And if anyone does not have the Spirit of Christ, he does not belong to Christ" (Romans 8:8-9 NIV).

Meanwhile, the flesh fights to maintain its position, folding under the pressure. I mean, really! Between dealing with your own desires, a wandering mind, the enticements of the world, and the whisperings of the devil, what's a poor little ball of puffed-up dust supposed to do? Those who suffer acutely from fear of falling do a religious jig that looks more like a poor imitation of the three little monkeys miming out "See no evil, hear no evil, say no evil." Another sector, one that embraces the grace of God but lacks the understanding of how that grace works, chooses to fall for one of the oldest deceptions that exists: "Well, I'll do it just this once and get it out of my system. After all, God will forgive me." Not realizing they are not getting anything out of their system, they are actually letting it *in*, stoking the fire beneath their desires.

Instead of using God's grace to strengthen their resolve to resist Temptation, they actually disregard it and abuse it instead. Is it the world dancing hypnotically like Herodias that makes us drunk with desire? Is it our own curiosity that propels us to see if how much of our own way we can have before we cross the line? Or was it the devil whispering to us that there won't be any serious consequences if God is as good as He says He is? The line of reasoning becomes very fuzzy, making it quite difficult to accuse any one entity of pushing a poor, sinful soul over the precipice of its own desire. And that is how Satan has designed it to work. He created the character in the red suit with the pitchfork, then gave him a lot of publicity. When the world became thoroughly convinced of that image of the devil, Satan exchanged his image for something more sophisticated, more unexpected— like a salesman in an expensive pinstriped suit. Real smooth.

After making his first major sale in the garden, Satan perfected his sales pitch down to a science. He presented his spiel to anyone who would listen, and it worked, too...until he ran into Jesus and tried the same routine on Him. You know the story: Jesus had been fasting for forty days and forty nights, which made Satan think to himself, "Oh, this is going to be easy! All I have to do is pull out the ol' satisfy-the-flesh display and *cha-ching!* The deal will be closed in no time, especially if I challenge His identity. If He doesn't fall for the food I offer, perhaps He'll at least try to prove that He is indeed the Son of God come to earth." But, much to Satan's chagrin, Jesus waved away his presentation of stones that turn to bread and completely ignored the devil's challenge to validate His identity with the convicting reply, "Man shall not live by bread alone, but by every word of God" (Luke 4:4 NKJV).

"This is going to be harder than I thought!" Satan's mind raced. "Okay, forget the pride approach. Jesus obviously has no ego. What manner of man is this? No food...no ego..." He snapped his fingers. "Eureka! I've got it! What man can resist the opportunity to rule the world? After all, the earth originally belonged to Him, and I'm certain He remembers the heady taste of power. Surely He will want it back. That way, I could kill two birds with one stone. I can get a little worship out of this exchange, and we'll be even." Well, as it turned out, Jesus thought that was a ridiculous proposition, and—in Michelle paraphrase—said, "Get outta here! What would I look like worshiping you? You know what the Word says: 'Thou shalt worship the Lord thy God, and him only shalt thou serve'" (Matthew 4:10 KJV).

"Man, this dude is a hard nut to crack!" For a moment Satan was stymied, but he recovered quickly to make one last-ditch effort. "Okay," he mumbled under his breath, "perhaps the straight ego trip approach will work if I don't attach any other conditions to it." So he played his last card and once again appealed to Jesus for proof of godly sonship. Jesus read him like a billboard. I like the Amplified version of Luke 4:12-13: "And Jesus replied to him, [the Scripture] says, You shall not tempt (try, test exceedingly) the Lord your God. [Deuteronomy 6:16.] And when the devil had ended every [the complete cycle of] temptation, he [temporarily] left Him [that is, stood off from Him] until another more opportune *and* favorable time."

I believe Satan was last seen muttering, "I need some time to regroup and try this again from another angle...hmmm, perhaps a plant in his camp will work. Yeah, I need someone to pull Him out of His ordained purpose. That's it!" And then a flicker of doubt creased his brow and his countenance darkened as his voice deepened to a venomous growl, "And if that doesn't work, then I'll just kill Him!"

So what was Jesus' secret? How did He overcome the devil in the face of such delectable enticements? Surely His flesh rose up and did a belly flop as He declined the opportunity to eat food after starving for forty days and forty nights. How many of us can bring ourselves to fast for one day before we're ready to feast on whatever is set before us, whether we like it or not? Surely the prospect of getting the world back at a steal of a deal (I mean, a harmless little show of worship—what's that?) should have had Jesus' adrenaline pumping. That is why He came to earth in the first place—to gain the world back. What a fabulous deal! He could skip whatever His agenda was and go straight to the ruling without passing "Go" and collecting 200 dollars. Quite a monopoly, so to speak. And who wouldn't want to make it absolutely clear that He was the Son of God, complete with light show and angels and everything, just to have the satisfaction of making a point? Perhaps we would, but Jesus didn't. And that brings me to a rather embarrassing conclusion about who the real culprit is in this temptation business.

To Tell the Truth

This whole scenario reminds me of a movie called *Big Business*. It was a story about two sets of twins who had been switched at birth and separated. One set ended up living in the country. They were everything sweet and pure and nice.

The other set grew up in the city and became ruthless business tycoons. In other words, their environments made them as different as day and night. As circumstances would have it, fate reunited them. Of course, it was a great shock to the system of one set to exit from two parallel bathroom stalls and run into one another. After going through a set of comical gyrations to see if the other was merely a mirror reflection, they finally realized the other face looking back at them was indeed another person. Upon this revelation they both began to scream hysterically. And so it is with us.

When we come to the Lord, we tend to believe we have been separated from that part of ourselves that is not everything sweet and pure and nice. And for a short time we are on such a high, such a wonderful honeymoon with the Lord, that we can take or leave the world and all it has to offer. And Satan does with us exactly what he did with Jesus. He retreats and waits for a more opportune time. He relies on the old adage that "what goes up usually comes down," and so he waits. Then one day we come out of the bathroom stall and run into ourself—the self we knew before the new birth, before the separation. And we are horrified. "How could this be happening?" we cry. "Surely the devil and the world have conspired against me!" But, in truth, in order to be their victim, we must be a willing one.

This, in part, is why Jesus overcame and we don't. (Jesus' divine nature is an additional factor, but He *did* have choices, and He chose not to give in to temptation.) This is why Satan accuses us. He knows that even though he is the tempter, the choice to deny or give in to temptation is ultimately up to us now that the divine nature of Christ abides in us. He still attempts to pull us backward by appealing to our sense of self-preservation.

This is why Satan tried to use Peter to dissuade Jesus from going to the cross. He tried to use others to persuade Jesus that He should forget this whole Savior thing and instead become a mighty leader who freed the Jews from the cruel arm of the Roman Empire. Why should He sacrifice Himself when He could live and be a hero? They encouraged Him to get caught up in the political and moral issues of the day. Satan desperately tried everything he could come up with to appeal to Jesus' sense of self-preservation. But Jesus knew He was not His own to preserve. He knew that "whosoever shall seek to save his life shall lose it; and whosoever shall lose his life shall preserve it" (Luke 17:33 KJV). And so Jesus ignored all the outward stimuli, centered Himself, and tried to help the others around Him comprehend what He was all about by being honest. I imagine Him telling them, "Hey, my heartbeat is to do the will of My Father who sent Me. Nothing else really matters. Nothing else will profit Me where I'm going. I am merely passing through on a very specific assignment, and then I'm out of here." But those around Him just didn't get it.

Oh, if only we could get it! (That is, get a grip on our purpose and stay focused.) It would affect our reaction to temptation, and we would find ourselves echoing the words of Jesus and saying, "Hey, I'm on a mission. I don't have time for that." People who keep their eyes focused on where they are going get in a lot less trouble than those who wander aimlessly. But, instead, most of us meander through life with no particular destination in mind. These are the people temptation lures to the side of the road to sample appetizers because they have no idea what's for dinner. By the time they somehow manage to reach their destination—which happens sheerly out of God's determination to complete His purposes—their appetite for the fine spread is ruined because of the bitter taste sin has left in their mouths. And Satan rubs his hands together in delight and whispers his favorite words: "It's all your fault!" And he's right.

It's All in How You Finish

There's something to be said for crossing the finish line in a blaze of glory as opposed to barely scraping your body over the chalk. I realize some will just be grateful to have made it. But be honest: Do you really want to spend eternity with the memory of such a pathetic entrance into glory? If there were ever a time for ego, this is the moment to consider: "O death, where is thy sting? O grave, where is thy victory?" (1 Corinthians 15:55 KJV). This is the cry of a person who has finished their course and fulfilled their purpose in a burst of undeterred triumph. We all have the opportunity to do so. "His divine power has given us everything we need for life and godliness through our knowledge of him who called us by his own glory and goodness" (2 Peter 1:3 NIV).

So, sad to say, in a court of law, Satan would merely be cited as an instigator. Perchance the world would be charged as an accessory to the crime. But the person who would stand trial for the actual crime would be you. Temptation is sneaky that way. He is the friend who sets you up and leaves you standing in the line of fire alone. And your parents remind you every time, "I warned you not to hang out with him! You were warned, and you chose to do your own thing. Now you must suffer the consequences." Didn't you always think your parents had eyes in the back of their head when things like that happened? How did they always know? Sounds like God to me, but in this case He says, "I gave you everything you need to overcome temptation—use it."

4

WHERE FOOLS
DARE TO TREAD

"And lead us not into temptation…"

MATTHEW 6:13 NIV

WE HAVE ALL HAD OUR OWN brushes with this mysterious stranger called Temptation, if we move under the premise that evil is not *something* but *someone*. I have my own personal testimony. I met Temptation one hot and sultry night as I meandered down the avenue of wandering thoughts and mindless escapes. It seemed as if he had appeared out of nowhere, materializing before me at the precise moment I grew indecisive about which direction to turn. He moved smoothly and silently toward me, his every step suggestive in nature, his entire being literally vibrating with the promise of an intriguing proposition. I was fascinated—and probably sold—even before the conversation began. Long, lean, and seductive, he possessed a voice potent with all that a restless soul craved. His eyes were deep, dark, and shiny as the marbles I bartered with as a child. In those eyes I saw the reflection of my most secret desires. I was transfixed, mesmerized, hypnotized by the aspect of being so close to that which I longed to possess. "It's yours for the taking," his musical voice whispered, soft as an inviting caress. "No one will ever know," he assured me. "It will be our little secret." His fingers closed around my arm, paralyzing my resistance as he led me away—willingly or unwillingly, I could not say. I found his stare far too riveting to shift my gaze, until I felt myself falling...falling into the abyss of disobedience.

The initial stage of my descent was actually pleasant to my senses as I felt the cool breeze of consummation on my flesh. Suddenly pain ripped throughout my entire being as I crashed upon a rock. Suspended in time by the shock of such an abrupt jolt back to unclouded awareness, the depths of my collision slowly dawned on me with each wave of fresh agony. With my spirit—as well as my fall—now broken, I lifted a hand for Temptation to help me regain solid footing, but he had vanished, leaving me to be scoffed at and ridiculed by unforgiving accusers.

I am sure this is how Samson felt after his experience with Delilah. I'm sure you have your own story to tell of an encounter with Temptation, but Samson's account has got to be one of the most tragic tales recounted in the Bible. That one so strong could be so weak is disconcerting. Even more disturbing is the fact that one who could have saved many from their oppressors died prematurely at their hands instead because of his own lack of discipline. His own refusal to heed the counsel of his parents led him down a path of no return. It reminds me of an important lesson I received very early in my childhood. A treasured friend of mine had been told he could not attend a neighborhood party while his parents were out for the evening. Friends stopped by and encouraged him to go to the party for just a few minutes, telling him he would be back home before his parents could find out anything. He was persuaded to go. Shortly after his arrival at the party, someone in the room began playing with a gun. A shot was fired accidentally, and the bullet ricocheted off the ceiling, catching this young man above the eye and killing him instantly.

My young friends and I were deeply affected by the needless death of one so young with such a promising future. Doesn't it always seem to happen to the brightest and the best? It's almost as if Satan glimpses into their future and sees something bright hovering there, and, in his intense hatred of all that God purposes to do, he devises a way to snuff out the light before it reaches the full potential of its brilliance.

More than thirty years later I can still feel the sense of despair that swept over me as I heard the news about my friend. A youth center was built in his name, and, last I heard, his sister still cries out his name as she weeps in church. The scars of his loss remain. And what of the things he was almost certain to accomplish as he grew to manhood? They remain unfinished by his hands. I'm sure someone else has filled the gap in his own way, but it certainly isn't the same as if it had been accomplished by the one who was created for that specific mission.

Misery Loves Company

There's one thing that we often forget as we respond to the voice of Temptation—Temptation has no respect for wisdom. He cares nothing for the specifics of your calling or your potential. He has no respect for God or His plans, and does everything in his power to make you displace yours. Temptation is like the strange woman in the book of Proverbs who has way too much time on her hands: "The lips of an immoral woman are as sweet as honey, and her mouth is smoother than oil. But the result is as bitter as poison, sharp as a double-edged sword. Her feet go down to death; her steps lead straight to the grave. For she does not care about the path to life. She staggers down a crooked trail and doesn't even realize where it leads" (Proverbs 5:3-6 NLT).

Solomon goes on to warn: "Run from her! Don't go near the door of her house! If you do, you will lose your honor and hand over to merciless people everything you have achieved in life. Strangers will obtain your wealth, and someone else will enjoy the fruit of your labor. Afterward you will groan in anguish when disease consumes your body, and you will say, 'How I hated discipline! If only I had not demanded my own way! Oh, why didn't I listen to my teachers? Why didn't I pay attention to those who gave me instruction? I have come to the brink of utter ruin, and now I must face public disgrace'" (Proverbs 5:8-14 NLT).

What would make a woman lead a man to such depths? Obviously, she had already lost all that she valued, had already been regarded as an embarrassment and disappointment to her husband, had already been looked upon by her neighbors as one to be despised. Only a person who has nothing to lose would invite someone else on such a despairing journey. Misery loves company indeed.

Remember, Temptation is already doomed to a fiery pit throughout eternity. Therefore, he would love to make life as miserable as possible for you—literally hell on earth—here and now. And so he entices you to forsake knowledge and discretion, to misplace counsel and sound judgment, to lose your understanding and your power. Yes, Temptation specializes in making you forgetful. Common sense goes out the window in one fatal swoop. Clear rationale becomes a thing of the past. And yet God's Word does not budge: "Can a man scoop fire into his lap without his clothes being burned? Can a man walk on hot coals without his feet being scorched?" (Proverbs 6:27-28 NIV). The consequences remain the same, but what does Temptation care? Your cooperation signals the completion of his mission. A little bruised and tattered from too many close brushes with your tantalizing friend? Sounds like a personal problem to him.

Temptation likes to get personal, likes to hit below the belt, so to speak. What else could reduce a man as strong as Samson to becoming putty in some deceitful woman's hands? In *The Works of Josephus,* the ancient Jewish historian Josephus states, "And indeed this man [Samson] deserves to be admired for his courage and strength, and magnanimity at his death, and that his wrath against his enemies went so far as to die himself with them. But as for his [Samson's] being snared by a woman, that is to be ascribed to human nature, which is too weak to resist the temptation to that sin; but we ought to bear him witness, that in all other respects he was one of extraordinary virtue."

I'm not sure I agree with all of that. Samson had some other flaws that opened the door for Temptation to come right in, get comfortable, and set up shop. Samson was a fool, plain and simple. Why? "A fool despiseth his father's instruction" (Proverbs 15:5 KJV). Samson's self-possessed nature led him to go to all the wrong places, touch all the wrong things, listen to all the wrong people, and commit all the wrong actions. I tend to believe that the few things he did right, he did purely by accident, yet God got the good out of them. But Samson was never disciplined enough to fulfill the will of God on purpose.

The Path of No Return

Perhaps Samson should not bear the full blame for his self-indulgent nature. I think the die was cast when Manoah and his wife had Samson in their old age. Having a memorable experience with the angel of the Lord, who came to announce their son's birth, didn't lessen their awe of this very special child, though they asked for instructions on how to raise him. I wonder if they stuck to the program. Was he merely strong-willed? Or did they spoil him? The bottom line was that he had no respect for authority.

So Samson went *down* to Timnah...*down* being the operative word here. *Down* to the wrong neighborhood, where he spotted the *wrong* kind of girl from the *wrong* side of the tracks. "Get her for me!" he insisted to his parents when he returned home. If Samson had grown up in my neighborhood, that would have been the end of the story right then and there. He would have spent the rest of his life looking for his teeth on the floor. In my view, Samson got off lightly. His parents' entreaties for him to choose a wife from among his own people fell on deaf ears. He had decided this fine-looking woman was the one for him. He hadn't spoken to her yet, but she appeared right in his eyes. Right for what? That's my question! At any rate, Samson felt no great need to heed his parents' advice—or even to respectfully consider it.

Whatever happened to "Honor your parents that things may go well with you and you may have long life?" (see Ephesians 6:2-3). Clearly, the converse of that passage is obvious. If you don't honor your parents, things won't go well with you and your life will be cut short. Obviously, this meant nothing to Samson. Perhaps he considered himself the exception to the rule. Ever felt invincible? That's a dangerous feeling, one that Samson probably knew well. So Samson beat his manly chest and ignored his parents. They compromised to keep the peace and succumbed to their son's demands, while God—foreknowing Samson's bad temper—chose to use the whole situation to His advantage and to further His own plans.

So many of us are guilty of this. We meet someone that we like, or encounter an opportunity that looks perfect to us. Others around us who are not wearing rose-colored glasses voice their reservations and we grow defensive, spurning their advice. Yet the Bible tells us, "Where no counsel is, the people fall: but in the multitude of counselors there is safety" (Proverbs 11:14 KJV). After some great disappointment or heartbreak, we usually find that those around us were accurate in their assessment, and we pray they won't utter those dreaded words, "I told you so." Oh, if only we would learn to embrace sound counsel from those who are wise and love us! This is one of the secrets to overcoming Temptation. Accountability and transparency with a grounded inner circle who can speak into our lives can keep us out of his clutches.

The sad thing about these types of situations is that rebellion and disobedience never affect just one person. They rub off on everyone related or close to the perpetrator. So, returning to Samson's story, the next thing we see is Samson's parents going *down* to Timnah, too! Samson's bringing everybody down, and not just physically. Not only does he have his parents wandering into the wrong neighborhood, forced to mingle with undesirables. He also begins violating the law of God right and left, literally every step of the way.

Samson became secretive. He killed a lion on the way and never mentioned it to his parents. Later, as he returned to claim his bride, he stopped to view his handiwork and found that bees had made a nest in the lion's carcass. He scooped up some honey from their honeycomb, ate it, and gave some to his parents to eat as well, being quite careful not to tell them the source of his offering. He was no longer accountable to or transparent with anyone. He had become like a child who falls and soils his outfit. Samson was now determined to soil the garments of all within his vicinity, hoping that he wouldn't look so dirty in comparison.

Now let me get this straight. I thought that, according to Levitical law, touching dead things was a violation that rendered one unclean. Yet instead of repenting and going in search of a guilt offering, Samson chose to soil others—namely, his parents—and use the entire experience to further his own gain by making it a riddle at his wedding. Those who couldn't solve the riddle would pay the groom with linen garments. This infuriated the guests, who, in turn, threatened to kill the new bride and everyone in her family's household if she didn't find out the answer from her husband and give it to them.

This is where Temptation rubbed his hands together in glee at the prospect of having such an open vessel to manipulate. He wrapped Samson's young bride around his finger and played her like a fine violin. He tuned her up and brought his bow down slowly. "You don't love me," she cried in high C. "If you did, you would tell me the answer to the riddle." At first Samson resisted, but by the seventh day the repetition of her tune had reduced him to weary carelessness, so he spilled the beans. And she quickly scooped them into her hands and fed them to her hungry people. The temper tantrum that Samson threw after the wedding guests had burst his bubble by solving the riddle was a murderous rampage—not a pretty sight. And then he stomped off, interestingly enough, up to his father's house.

So let's recap this drama for a minute here. Samson opens the play by going *down* to Timnah and finding a girl he wants. He then takes his parents *down* with him. He goes *down* to speak with the girl he saw there. His father goes *down* to see the woman, everyone goes *down* to the wedding, and after all is said and done—with quite tragic results—Samson returns to his senses and goes *up* to his father's house...ver-r-r-y interesting! I pray that if you've fallen down you will have the determination to look *up* to your heavenly Father for restoration.

The Patience of Temptation

One would think that Samson could breathe a sigh of relief now that he had returned to his correct position. But, unfortunately, that relief would be only short-lived. Temptation merely bided his time, knowing that, true to his nature, Samson would not be able to let sleeping dogs lie. Knowing that Samson's bride had been given away—and that this could provoke another murderous display from the volatile man—Temptation leaned over his prey, blowing his cool breath in Samson's face, and hissed, "You know you have needs. Why not visit that lovely little wife of yours? After all, you owe it to yourself to get some delight out of all this misery." On that note, Temptation stepped back to view his handiwork. "It won't be long now," he chuckled to himself.

Sure enough, once Samson discovered that his bride had been given away behind his back, he set off to wreak havoc in the fields of the Philistines and put his fellow countrymen at risk. But somehow, in the midst of Samson's seeming compulsion toward disaster and devastation, the situation ended up working "to the good" as Samson routed the Philistines. Not exactly what Temptation had in mind! Sure, a few battles had been won on behalf of the kingdom of darkness, but the war itself remained unresolved at this point. However, Temptation knew that it was simply a matter of time. It was obvious that Samson hadn't learned a thing from his experiences.

Third Encounters of the Foolish Kind

Delilah is the leading character in the *third* recorded encounter that Samson had with women from the wrong side of the tracks. What was it about those Philistine women that Samson just couldn't get enough of, anyway? Was he merely "acting out" because he knew how much his Philistine adventures disturbed his parents, or did he delight in the thrill of plucking forbidden fruit? Perhaps these Philistine women provided just the escape Samson needed. They never nagged him about his Levitical vows; they had no standard of holiness by which to uphold Samson. He could drop by, enjoy a glass of wine, and not face a disapproving stare.

At any rate, Samson ended up living in the valley of Sorek with a harlot named Delilah. (There he goes...*down* again.) At this point, Samson had totally lost it. He had lost all regard for the law of God. He was marked at birth for the priest-hood, he was a judge in Israel, yet he gave no thought to how he looked before the nation or God. Still, he expected the protection of God. That is pure, unadulterated nerve! I believe it's safe to say that Samson had entered into full-blown rebellion at this stage in the game. Paul warned that "in the latter times some shall depart from the faith, giving heed to seducing spirits...having their conscience seared with a hot iron" (1 Timothy 4:1-2 KJV). Paul goes on to give a list of the things people would do in the name of religion.

Though Samson was in rebellion, he held on to a form of religion. However, his faith was misplaced—his faith was in his hair, in the outward manifestation of what should have been an inner conviction. But rebellion will always dull our senses. Samson's relationships with women were just like his relationship with God—totally on his terms, for his own con-venience. He didn't bother to truly communicate with the women, and he most certainly did not communicate with God. Unless he wanted something, that is.

Samson spoke to God the same way he spoke to his par-ents. After winning a battle against the Philistines, he bragged about himself, giving no honor to God. After growing thirsty, he cried out to the Lord, "You have accomplished this great victory *by the strength of your servant*. Must I die now of thirst in the hands of these pagan people?" (see Judges 15:18). Can you imagine? Temptation had done his job well. He had Samson believing his own press. But God is not mocked, and He certainly cannot be ordered around. Perhaps the most awesome thing about God is that He is even more patient than Temptation. Sure enough, as the old saying goes, every dog has its day.

The Art of Seduction

With his senses as dull as an overused knife, his discernment completely gone by the wayside, Samson lands in the arms of Delilah—"Dee-lie-yah," as some have called her. Her name itself reeks of seduction. It literally rolls off the tongue, doesn't it? Provoked by the leaders of the Philistines as well as her own greed for a hefty reward, she dripped honey all over Samson. What she did to him could have been called nagging, if it hadn't been done in such an artful manner. "Tell me the secret of your strength," she crooned. I'm sure this was after she had rendered him completely vulnerable with her charms, if you know what I'm talking about. And he, being a bit drowsy and inebriated with all of her womanly ministrations, but not totally out of his mind yet, decided to humor her with a lie in order to placate her for the evening. After all, he had every intention of revisiting this well.

Here's where the plot thickens and you wonder why the star didn't get it. It's like watching a scary movie when the music changes and you know the monster is preparing to pounce. You sit in your chair cringing in anxiety-ridden anticipation of the worst while the star marches onward toward the danger, completely unaware. Well, Delilah tested Samson's response, and found out he was merely teasing her when the Philistines pounced, only to find him just as physically strong as ever. But Delilah was a determined woman, so she didn't give up. Next she stepped up the art of manipulation by inflicting guilt on Samson, hoping that this would keep him defending himself long enough not to notice that she was the traitor in the scenario. She was the one who betrayed his confidence, yet he found himself apologizing for lying to her! Truly a stroke of Temptation's genius. He covers his tracks well.

I don't know what Delilah was putting in Samson's stew, but it must have been truly potent. I can't think of anyone I know who would stick with someone who betrayed him to life-threatening proportions three times in a row. Yet Samson kept coming back for more of whatever it was that she was serving up. But, as in any good game, there are a set number of violations before a player gets disqualified. The problem is, in the game of life we never know how many violations we're allowed. Some get more chances than others, some get less. In Samson's case, God finally got tired of the game and the referee called the contest. At last, Delilah got the secret out of Samson.

Temptation exhaled as Samson told her the secret of his strength: "'My hair has never been cut,' he confessed, 'for I was dedicated to God as a Nazirite from birth. If my head were shaved, my strength would leave me, and I would become as weak as anyone else'" (Judges 16:17 NLT). I'm shocked that he still remembered his purpose! But his explanation reveals a lot. Samson's faith was definitely misplaced. His understanding of how God operated was completely off. I mean, come on, I know that men are really into their hair, but this is ridiculous! Let's talk about this hair thing for a moment. To this day it seems that many men link their desirability, virility, and self-confidence directly to their hair. The creators of Rogaine, toupees, and flourishing hair clubs attest to the fact that men take their hair—and the growth of it—very seriously. But what is the significance of hair, scripturally speaking? Well, in 1 Corinthians 11:7 Paul says, "A man should not wear anything on his head when worshiping, for man is God's glory, made in God's own image, but woman is the glory of man" (NLT). Strangely enough, he states that it is disgraceful for a man to have long hair (see 1 Corinthians 11:14) and that a woman's hair is her glory (see 1 Corinthians 11:15). So what happened between the book of Judges and where Paul now stood? And how could Samson possibly have drawn strength from his hair alone if God was into shifting hair trends?

What is this "glory thing" all about? God's glory is His power and His presence made manifest in answer to our obedience and praise. Remember, Satan wants that glory. Temptation has been assigned to diffuse the glory of God. His job is to tarnish man's shiny halo, take his glow down a hundred notches, or better yet, snuff it out completely. Of course, Samson didn't know any of that and, lacking knowledge, he erred greatly by relying on the wrong source for his power.

Samson missed the truth that his hair was merely an outward symbol of his life set apart for God's glory. There it is! Plain and simple. Between the Book of Judges and 1 Corinthians, Jesus came on the scene and set a few things in order. Now God became man's direct covering, reflecting His glory directly through the life of every man who is submitted to Him. And man became the covering for the woman in like fashion. The woman's hair was now seen as an outward show of her femininity and her being set apart for the man who covered her. Paul was explaining that this outward display (long, uncut hair) was no longer necessary. The concept of being set apart had become an attitude of the heart, with no more need to rely on religious symbolism. Yet even today churches start traditions that have absolutely no foundation in godly or scriptural principle. They're all based on what good ol' grandpa did and what his father did and what his father's father did, and so on. Samson never got it. He actually believed he was operating on his own power, thanks to his hair. He didn't give God any credit.

The Lap of the Tempter

So Delilah cooked up her special brand of Seduction Soup, and Samson slurped it down and fell asleep in her lap. Bad move. Whatever you do, avoid the lap of the devil. A preacher friend of mine once said, "If you go to sleep in the lap of the devil, don't expect to wake up in the bosom of Abraham." The devil always has a pair of scissors in his hand. He's always up for a good haircut. He delights in those buzz cuts. You know the type—the kind that cuts destinies short and lops off purpose. You know how you feel after a bad haircut. It can be completely debilitating to stare at the reflection of yourself in the mirror and see a familiar face with strange-looking hair staring back at you. Kinda throws you off, doesn't it? Makes you feel slightly powerless. You can't quite seem to function in your usual rhythm until you get used to the new you. Your only comfort is, "Oh well, it's only hair. It'll grow back." Unfortunately, Samson did not have that luxury in his situation. His haircut cost him more than a few compliments. It cost him his eyesight, his freedom, and eventually his life. Yes, when Samson—totally unaware of his lady friend's handiwork—awoke from his self-satisfied fog with the Philistines descending upon him, the Bible says that he assumed he would do what he had always done: "When he woke up, he thought, 'I will do as before and shake myself free.' But he didn't realize the LORD had left him. So the Philistines captured him and gouged out his eyes. They took him to Gaza, where he was bound with bronze chains and made to grind grain in the prison" (Judges 16:20-21 NLT).

Samson experienced the work of Temptation at its finest. Temptation was completely successful in lulling Samson into a place of rebellious numbness, misplaced religion, and insensitivity to the Spirit of God. Temptation led him straight into the arms of Deception, who robbed him of his discernment, cut off his strength, blinded him, put him in bondage, and reduced him to existing in the basement, living beneath his calling. I can picture Temptation dusting off his hands in satisfaction while his cohorts in darkness cheered him and gave him high fives.

In spite of Temptation's seeming victory, God had his own agenda that He was determined to fulfill. And so He used the time of Samson's imprisonment to teach him where the true source of his strength came from. Samson's hair grew back, and as he was led out to be sport for one of the Philistine festivals, he prayed, "Sovereign LORD, remember me again. O God, please strengthen me one more time so that I may pay back the Philistines for the loss of my eyes" (Judges 16:28 NLT).

I'm not sure that was the motive Samson should have had after such a painful lesson, but right now we'll take whatever we can get. And so one final time the Spirit of the Lord visited Samson and he destroyed the temple, killing the Philistines gathered there and himself. The Bible says that he killed more Philistines in his death than he had during his entire lifetime, but the fact remains that this was an unnecessary ending that affected many others besides himself.

The Israelites didn't need a mass murderer of the Philistines as much as they needed a judge who would lead them out of captivity. Samson's last coup was a mere Band-Aid, when what the nation really needed was a cure. Instead, the Israelites' land remained in a state of being seemingly incurable. The actions of Samson cost them dearly. And how much more could he have accomplished alive? But Samson stepped off the road of destiny to dance with Temptation at the ball. The clock struck twelve, the stagecoach turned into a pumpkin, and he was never able to retrace his steps back home. His disobedience cost him the umbrella of God's protection, and he got drenched by the consequences of his own bad decisions.

These were the consequences Solomon alluded to in the book of Proverbs when warning his son about the dangers of yielding to the invitations of seductive and adulterous women. "These commands are a lamp, this teaching is a light, and the corrections of discipline are the way to life, keeping you from the immoral woman, from the smooth tongue of the wayward wife. Do not lust in your heart after her beauty or let her captivate you with her eyes, for the prostitute reduces you to a loaf of bread, and the adulteress preys upon your very life. Can a man scoop fire into his lap without his clothes being burned? Can a man walk on hot coals without his feet being scorched?" (Proverbs 6:23-28; see also Proverbs 7:7-27). This is advice that every man or woman should heed. Beware of the man or woman who lures you off the path of right-standing with God. Don't allow your ego to be stroked with their smooth words and tantalizing ways. They are only trying to fulfill their own selfish agenda, which does not include preserving your heart, your life, or your well-being, either physically or spiritually. They will leave you in the rubble of your self-destruction without a backward glance after they have had their way with you.

The Hidden Price Tag

One day my father was counseling a convict at the correctional facility where he is employed. He sat and listened to the convict relate the story of how he had come to be incarcerated. The man had spent the night with a prostitute, and he decided not to pay her because he didn't think she was good enough to earn the twenty-five dollars she was charging him. The prostitute then accused the man of raping her. He was convicted and landed in jail. My father then asked the man to compare his sentence of seven to fifteen years with the twenty-five dollars he owed the woman, and to tell him if it was worth it. And so it is with the momentary pleasure we reap from satisfying the "lust of the flesh." This is what Temptation knows but you must find out. He slithers ahead of you to hide the price tag.

In the book of Genesis, Reuben was denied the blessing of the firstborn because he just had to have his father's wife. His short-lived self-indulgence cost him a lasting legacy—the blessing of his father. In the world we presently occupy, we hear countless stories of people suffering public disgrace and demotion because of the revelation of sexual sin or adulterous flings. Careers and benefits, life partners, respect, and all that they have labored for have disintegrated before their very eyes while the world watches and openly debates their personal business. The true irony of it all emerges. The ones who lead them to their fall seem to not only profit from the whole scandal, but are celebrated as well. They make their money from interviews and books about it all and then settle into a seemingly peaceful existence away from the glaring spotlight, while the "victims" are left holding nothing, their lives in shambles.

If you don't know your enemy's agenda, you will always play into his hands. So understand and know that Temptation is out to abort, destroy, and completely annihilate your purpose along with any evidence of it. He is out to steal your blessing. He stands ready with his cutting shears poised, waiting for you to settle into his lap.

Funny thing about hairdressers. They always know and easily recognize their handiwork. They know when you've been unfaithful and wandered off to try someone else's salon. According to Matthew 10:30, God has numbered every hair on your little head. He delights in surveying His handiwork, and He grieves when we allow others to rearrange what He so carefully designed to reflect His glory. And, like a good hairdresser, He knows when you've been sitting in someone else's chair. Don't allow Temptation to lure you away in pursuit of a special offer that you can't resist. Ultimately, you'll have to crawl back to God to repair the damage. Sometimes He will, sometimes He won't. Wake up and be aware. Is anybody cutting your hair?

5

WHERE WISE MEN STUMBLE

"But every person is tempted when he is drawn away,
enticed and baited by his own evil desire..."

JAMES 1:14 AMP

WHERE EXACTLY DOES THE TROUBLE BEGIN? The answer is quite basic. The trouble begins with our own appetites, our own "needs." I cringe at that word because many things that we call "needs" are merely strong "wants." Temptation plays upon our inability to discern the difference, dangling carrots inches from our noses until it becomes almost impossible to refuse them. Temptation's arm never grows tired of holding the object of our desire close enough for us to reach but far away enough to make us stumble when we grasp it.

I've seen trouble coming many times. I've felt myself losing my footing along a slippery way. All the alarms were sounding in my head, but my feet seemed to have a mind of their own. Yet, at the end of the day, I could not say it wasn't my fault when I was faced with the consequences of my actions. Years later, after several relationships that ended quite painfully, I honestly had to admit that I had no one to blame but myself for the state in which I found myself. All the warning signs had been there from the beginning, yet I chose to ignore them and fling myself heartfirst into relationships I instinctively knew were doomed to go nowhere. In the end, all I could do was sigh and scold myself for choosing temporary indulgence over self-discipline. Eventually I learned that this was not the best method for maturing gracefully. In an age where everyone justifies their wrongdoing by outrightly shirking responsibility or blaming present mistakes on past "sins of the fathers," there was no justification for my saying yes in the face of God's resounding no.

The Cost of Disobedience

Like a character in my favorite children's book, *When We Were Very Young* by A.A. Milne, I, too, overestimated my power to rebound after dancing too close to the edge of the cliff. In the poem "Disobedience," James James Morrison Morrison Whetherby George DuPree admonished his mother not to go down to the end of the town without consulting him. Well, as the story goes, she then dressed herself up in a golden gown and reasoned that she could venture down to the end of the town and be back in time for tea. Poor dear, she was never seen or heard of again. After an extensive search that was orchestrated by the king himself, he was overheard telling one of his subjects, "Well, when people go 'down' to the end of the town, then what can anyone do?" There's that word *down* again!

I found the notice that was posted all over town in an attempt to locate the missing mother quite interesting and telling of most who fall even today. It read:

> Lost, or stolen or strayed,
> James James Morrison's mother

seems to have been mislaid.
Last seen wandering aimlessly,
quite of her own accord,
She tried to get down
to the end of the town—forty shillings reward!"[3]

Yes, it is the wandering "aimlessly quite of our own accord" that gets us into trouble. This is where the best-laid traps of Temptation are set. He knows that timing is everything. What is it that entices us to make wrong choices against our better instincts or intellectual knowledge? It is a "need" that has become urgent.

Timing Is Everything

Place a steak in front of a dog and stand back to watch what happens. If the dog isn't hungry, he can take it or leave it. But when that dog is ravenous, he will attack the steak with relish, without a sniff, even if it isn't generally his favorite thing to eat.

Temptation knows that his work isn't just to wave a tempting morsel in front of us. He must wave it at the right time—the time when we become acutely aware of a void within us, an overwhelming "need" that begins to spread like a fire throughout our being. This is when Temptation steps in—at the moment when we would do anything to put the fire out, we blindly reach for a pail of water and he hands us gasoline. And as the flames grow ever higher to the point of being out of control, we stand in awe of the blazing inferno, too hypnotized to call the fire department.

I believe timing was crucial in the saga of David and Bathsheba. As a matter of fact, the Bible states that "the following spring, the time of year when kings go to war, David sent Joab and the Israelite army to destroy the Ammonites. In the process they laid siege to the city of Rabbah. But David stayed behind in Jerusalem" (2 Samuel 11:1 NLT). So the story starts with David out of position, which is always a place of vulnerability. David stayed at home while the rest of his people went off to battle.

How many times do we find ourselves resting out of season, taking a nap when we should be engaged in spiritual warfare over the situations in our lives? We feel a void when everyone else is busy doing what they should be doing and we are not. Ever decided to stay home when your friends or family went somewhere, only to find yourself bored and wishing you had gone with them after they departed? This is when the "wandering aimlessly" begins. You had no specific plans, no specific reason for staying home. You just didn't feel like going at the time. But now that everyone is gone, what should you do with yourself? You don't feel like doing anything in particular...hmm, perhaps you need a nap.

Many have taken naps and let their guard down in a moment of weariness. They've settled for momentary comfort only to find it had lasting consequences. Such as the man or woman who finds themselves in an uneventful marriage. The passion is gone. They feel their needs are no longer met by their spouse. After trying to relight the fire to no avail, they've settled into accepting life as it is. They've taken a nap, no longer willing to fight to make their marriage work. Enter stage left another lonely soul having problems in their own marriage, or a vulnerable single person with an open ear. After exchanging intimate information that should be shared only with their spouse, a bond of intimacy forms with their "understanding friend," an affair is ignited, and a marriage is destroyed—simply because they rested with the wrong person.

Well, as they say, "An idle mind is the devil's workshop." And so David took a nap, physically and spiritually. After he rose from his nap he decided to take a stroll on the rooftop, and in his wanderings his eyes landed on a voluptuous sight—that of Bathsheba bathing. Perhaps he had seen her or other women bathing on the rooftop from his palace perch before, but this evening was different. This evening David had a nagging need, and Temptation had an appeasement. What could the need have been? David had seven wives already and countless concubines! You mean to tell me David could not have selected some little pretty from those who already belonged to him to indulge himself? Speaking of things that make you go *hmm!*

The Disguise of Deception

I find it necessary to say here that Temptation does not usually hand you what you need to hit the spot. He hands you an illusion of gratification. Overweight people are not overeating because they crave food. Their need comes from a deeper place. Food merely becomes the substitute which reaches the itch that cannot be scratched, so to speak. Before I came to the Lord I smoked cigarettes. Those awful, smelly little sticks were like a sedative in times of stress, a stimulant when I was weary, a snack when I was hungry. You could never convince me that I was addicted until I tried to quit. I truly enjoyed a good cigarette; it was comforting, it was relaxing, it was like taking a deep breath. It was...well, you get the picture. From time to time, even after coming to Christ and releasing my nicotine habit, I found myself longing for a good cigarette in moments of stress.

At times I even dreamed of smoking, and then halfway through the cigarette I would come to myself and in horror put it out. Now, it wasn't really a cigarette that I needed. It was a deeper need for comfort or inner stimuli that I was unable to grasp. A cigarette merely became my pacifier to silence the cry from within. Many who stop smoking find themselves battling weight gain as they increase their intake of food to placate what has now become an oral fixation. It's a vicious cycle, this thing called conquering the flesh.

The Steps to Falling

At any rate, what happened to David after he indulged in being a Peeping Tom on his roof would be labeled *premeditated* in any court of law today. And Proverbs 6:16 lists seven things that are an abomination to God: a proud look, a lying tongue, hands that shed innocent blood, a heart that devises wicked imaginations, feet that are swift in running to do mischief, a false witness that speaks lies, and a person who sows discord among brethren. Well, in reviewing David's steps, I think he covered a couple of those. Needless to say, his moves were more calculated than impulsive and swift.

First, David inquired as to who exactly this beautiful woman was. I find his servant's response interesting: "Isn't this Bathsheba, the daughter of Eliam and the wife of Uriah the Hittite?" (2 Samuel 11:3 NIV). As if to hint, "You could not possibly be talking about *her!*" But indeed David was. The fact that she was a married woman was not enough to deter him. David had a "need," and no one else mattered.

The evidence of how an overwhelming need can rule out sound reasoning is apparent every time a parent or family member lists the articles stolen and exchanged for a little bag of white powder. Merciless, senseless robberies take place in order to wrench a mere pittance that enables an addict to buy their "fix." *Somebody please do something to silence the voices in my head, in my flesh, in my soul!* That's their real cry. Anyone standing between the need and the solution becomes a hindrance that must be, depending upon the situation, maneuvered around, ignored, or removed.

And so it was for David. "Yup, she's the one I want," he determined. On that note, he sent for her and slept with her. Truly, he could not say, "It just happened." There was a lot of protocol here. He had to summon the servant, point out which rooftop he had seen her on, have a conversation about her identity, call another set of servants to round up a messenger and dispatch them with transportation, then wait until they came back with her in tow. Meanwhile, he probably took a bath and got himself together for her visit. No, this did not by any stretch of the imagination just happen!

When God Is Forgotten

I am still intrigued by what it was that nagged David from deep within. How does a man who has the discernment and wisdom to determine not to kill a man like Saul stoop to such an all-time low? Saul had been seeking David's life in order to secure his role as king—a role that rightly belonged to David, according to God. Yet David passed up the opportunity to finish Saul off. It was such an absurd case of stalking that it might have been termed justifiable homicide if David had chosen to kill Saul. Everyone would have understood, and many would have cheered. But David trusted God to remove Saul and promote himself according to His divine timing. In *Story of Stories,* author Karen C. Hinckley makes a haunting statement: "David refused to try to take by force what Yahweh promised by grace."[4]

But with Bathsheba, David threw all obedience, caution, and grace to the wind. It's been said that men rarely reach for what they need, but they always reach for what they want. David wanted what he wanted, and that was the bottom line. So he sent for her, he slept with her, and God watched and said nothing. But one day a message came that let David know that this one-night stand was going to cost him for the rest of his life. Bathsheba was pregnant. With *his* child.

We sit horrified before our television sets as story after story unfolds of teenagers who, terror-stricken by their own pregnancies, kill their infants and discard them as if they were a school paper containing too many errors to be presented. Their unrepentant expressions throw us into complete befuddlement as we wonder what they were thinking and how they possibly could have done such a horrific deed. But fear makes us do foolish things, even at the expense of others.

So David thought, *This is easy enough,* while Temptation, urging him to cover his tracks, hissed, "What Uriah doesn't know won't hurt him." With Deception assisting David in devising a calculating ruse, David sent for Bathsheba's husband, Uriah, to return home. After being on the battlefield with a bunch of smelly men, surely the sight of his beautiful wife would stir his passions. Surely Uriah would indulge himself and never be the wiser that the child Bathsheba bore was not his own. After all, certainly he wouldn't have time to calculate the baby's conception when he was caught up in the heat of battle.

Temptation's Betrayal

Here is where Temptation showed his true nature as a horribly rotten friend. Though he urges us to cover our tracks, he doesn't assist us in this endeavor. Why didn't Temptation cause Uriah to take the bait? Because this particular episode was not about Uriah; it was about the destruction of David. So Uriah returned home and refused to sleep with his wife while his buddies were still fighting. This is when reality set in for David. This was serious. He could foresee the walls of his world tumbling down, and he could not allow this to happen. The next drastic step must be taken. His reputation and the kingdom must be preserved at all costs.

This was a far cry from David's prayer in Psalm 23:3: "He leads me in the paths of righteousness for His name's sake" (NKJV). God had been forgotten. This had nothing to do with God's reputation and everything to do with David's. Forgetting God always makes us irrational. Temptation knows that.

He delights in "driving us to distraction," so to speak. If he can orchestrate us running around in circles, never seeking the face of God in the messes we create for ourselves, it renders us completely impotent spiritually and naturally. Then not much can be said, except "Mission accomplished!" as we land splat in the midst of the mess we've created. Forgiven, yes, but with permanent stains on our clothing.

The Breeding Ground for Sin

Well, Uriah didn't take the bait. Perhaps this explains why Bathsheba was a seemingly willing participant in all of this. After all, nothing is recorded in the Bible about her resisting David's attempts to seduce her. No cry of "Rape!" No accusations of "sexual harassment," words that are quick to be tossed about today. No, Bathsheba was strangely silent until the fateful words "I am with child" were spoken from her lips. This is merely supposition, but perhaps she was a woman who had grown weary of being ignored and now longed for a little affection. And here was a king, handsome and romantic, whispering to her how beautiful she was. How long had she waited to hear those words from the lips of her own husband?

Perhaps Bathsheba had grown accustomed to the idea that her husband was a "good man," but lacking something in a few areas. "It's really not that important that he's not romantic and affectionate. At least he works hard and takes good care of me," she might have reasoned to herself. But in the face of unadulterated (pardon the pun) appreciation and seduction, she had melted and allowed herself to feel the pleasure of being appreciated as a woman in every sense of the word. And what about David? Bathsheba was the first woman noted in the Bible who really got David's attention. Michal was in love with him, so Saul gave her to him. David, however, was more taken with the idea of being the son-in-law of the king than the idea of being Michal's husband. He probably married Abigail because he felt obligated to preserve her well-being after her husband died. After all, she had very wisely kept David from making a terrible mistake in the heat of anger. And Ahinoam, Maacah, Haggith, Abital, and Eglah were probably more strategic alliances than romantic interests while David was in Hebron and after he became king.

As for any affection David might have felt for Michal, that was snuffed out when she despised him for dancing before the Lord. But even this action on her behalf revealed her as a bitter woman with a deeply wounded spirit. If you remember, Michal was the one who lied and protected David in order to help him escape and incurred the wrath of her father, Saul. She did all of this to win David's love and approval. After David fled the scene, Saul gave her away to another man. When David became king, he demanded she be returned. The Bible goes on to say in 2 Samuel 2:1-15 that her husband followed her, weeping, until he was turned back by Abner.

After Michal returned home to David, I'm sure things were never the same between them. He now had other wives. He probably couldn't get over the fact that she had been touched by another man, and he was most likely restrained if he had any dealings with her at all. She, in turn, felt rejected and remembered the days of having a husband who loved her. No palace surroundings could make up for the coldness she now felt. And, in her thoughts, here she was with a man who made a fool of himself in the streets over a God he could not see while his wife stood before him in the flesh and got no response. Small wonder she couldn't keep a lid on the venom she spewed out of the window that day! All of these circumstances lead me to believe that David's heart had not yet found a resting place, even though he was surrounded by women. Temptation knew this, and when it comes to putting needy birds of a feather together, you won't find a better matchmaker than Temptation.

And David? Well, he was wide open, a sitting target waiting to be hit, because he had violated a very basic law of God from the beginning. Deuteronomy 17:17 instructs that the king "must not take many wives, or his heart will be led astray" (NIV). Aha! No one thought about David's particular sin because it was socially acceptable. After all, he was a king! But God was not impressed with his title. Though He loved David's state of heart toward Him, He could not violate His own word by protecting David from the consequences of his sin. Temptation knew that, too. And Temptation stood before God, boldly proclaiming his right to wag Bathsheba under David's nose because he had violated this one little law. Let the chips fall where they may. Everyone would soon get to see what David was really made of.

It is the little doors, cracked open slightly, that get us in big trouble. It is unanswered needs that go unspoken to God or anyone else that leave room for Temptation to slip in. Our eyes and our ears are the openings that the enemy uses to worm his way into our hearts. The need to be wanted, desired, and embraced is not sin in itself, but it is if it becomes greater than our desire for God to fill the void. This innocent need becomes active fuel in the area of adultery. It is volatile when mixed with our emotions. I always advise singles not to listen to the marital problems of those who are struggling with their spouses. But the same advice applies to those who are unhappily married, even among Christians. Once Temptation gets your ear, his whisper becomes convincing: "This person needs you. You could be a better mate to them. They are just misunderstood. But *you* understand them...." On and on, he weaves perfectly reasonable-sounding instructions "You are the answer to their problem." Soon the perfectly well-meaning person, led on by their own desire for love, is caught in the snare of an adulterous affair that is sure to end in heartbreak—the death of a marriage and a family, the death of trust and self-respect.

When Sin Is Finished

And so the fateful words echo in our hearts after we've "done it." "Then, after desire has conceived, it gives birth to sin; and sin, when it is full-grown, gives birth to death. Don't be deceived, my dear brothers" (James 1:15-16 NIV). Poor Uriah! He never knew what hit him. He came home the hapless recipient of what most would consider an honor. Just think how you would feel: "Wow! The king wants to have dinner with me and ask of my welfare! He indulges me and sends me to visit my wife before going back to the battlefield!" But Uriah chose to sleep at the entrance of the palace instead of going home to his wife. And, in doing so, he signed his own death warrant. His refusal to sleep with his wife caused greater problems than he could imagine.

Talk about the maximum penalty for defrauding a spouse! If Uriah had slept with his wife, he would have lived. What a reward for having a sense of honor! But what type of honor was it, really? I think it's safe to say that Uriah was honorably wrong. His is the story of too many men in ministry as well as those in secular professions. The needs of their own house go unnoticed in the name of "taking care of business." The end result is deception, death, and destruction. And you thought there was only one guilty party in this story.

Running Ahead of God

Well, Uriah dies by David's order, and after Bathsheba's time of grieving is over, David sends for her and makes her his wife. I have often wondered to myself if God's ultimate plan was to bring David and Bathsheba together from the beginning. What would have happened if everyone had remained obedient and not run ahead of God? Bathsheba was in the lineage of Jesus Christ. Was that relationship not always a part of God's design? I'm sure God had very specific ideas of whom to include in that family tree, and that He knew it long before David decided to take a stroll on his rooftop. If indeed "the steps of the godly are directed by the LORD" (Psalm 37:23 NLT), and if indeed "[God's] work has been finished since the creation of the world" (Hebrews 4:3 NIV), then according to His Word, this is a legitimate question.

In His foreknowledge of all we would say and do, God designed the road map of our lives to handle the detours He knew we would take. He also equipped us with bumpers to eventually land us back on course, smack-dab in the center of His divine plan. We might arrive there with nicks and bruises, a bent heart, and a smashed-up spirit, but we arrive. Not ahead of time, not a second too late. Even before time began, God was the perfect host, anticipating everything His guests would do and standing in ready preparation.

Now let's look at this realistically. Let's rewind the tape and consider a different ending to the movie starring David and Bathsheba. David strolls out on the rooftop, looks around, and sees a beautiful woman bathing. He says to himself, "My, my, my, isn't she beautiful! Oh, well, bless the Lord. Let me go back to my room and worship God." He goes back inside and calls to one of his servants, "Hey, do you know of a beautiful lady who lives two rooftops over? Oh, she's Uriah's wife? The man who fights in my army? Well, isn't it a small world! Listen, please take some fruit and a nice juicy lamb over to her, and make sure she has everything she needs while her husband is away."

Time passes. Uriah gets killed in the war with no orchestration by David. The word gets back to David, and he says, "What? Uriah got killed? Well, blessed be the name of the Lord. Uriah fought a good fight. How is his widow doing?

Please check on her and make sure she has everything she needs. This must be a trying time for her."

More time passes. When Bathsheba's grieving period has passed, David notices that she remains in the house where he saw her. So he asks his servant, "How is Uriah's widow doing? I see no one has come to claim her. Is there no kinsman-redeemer on Uriah's side of the family? None? Hmm, why don't you invite her to join me for dinner?" And the rest is history. They end up getting together the right way, and David finishes his reign as brilliantly as he started it.

That would have been nice, wouldn't it? A little too nice for Satan's liking. You see, Satan cannot stop the purposes of God, so he tries his best to pervert and mar the squeaky-clean glow of God's divine plan. But somehow we triumph because of God's sovereignty and that one awesome statement: "We know that all things work together for good to them that love God, to them who are the called according to *his* purpose" (Romans 8:28 KJV, emphasis added).

God uses even our mistakes to lead us back to the right position in Him. How could all things work together for good if all things had not already been anticipated, accounted for, and compensated for? This is one of the great mysteries of our omniscient God. Romans 8:28 says all things—the word *all* means *all*; *all* is not a conditional word—will turn out for good. This Scripture does not lend itself to the philosophy that *some* things, according to the degree of the mistake, will turn out for good. It simply—and very decisively—says *all*. Again, I underscore "to them that love God," because those who have a heart for God, and ultimately long to please Him, choose to learn from the mistakes they make and become better people from the experience. So instead of waiting and enjoying a perfectly clean ending, David gave in to his "need" for immediate gratification behind door number two. He got a prize, but lost some valuable bonus prizes. Why couldn't he wait? Because he didn't trust God.

"Now wait a minute!" you say. "This is the same David who whipped Goliath. He was bold while grown soldiers trembled!" This is true. David had a successful track record with God when it came to fighting battles. But he hadn't been so successful in love. Love was a foreign country he had not conquered. So when he saw something he actually desired, he went for it; he didn't wait for God to deliver. After all, God had allowed his first bride to be given away. How could he possibly believe that God was able to keep the woman he wanted until the appointed time? Plus, the woman he wanted was married—he saw no legal way of having her. Am I stepping on anyone's toes?

David hadn't been privy to the discussions being held in heaven about how this whole thing was supposed to come together. But Satan had been. Rubbing his hands together, he said to himself, "Oh yeah? We'll see about that. Since I can't stop God's perfect little plan, I think I know exactly how to tarnish His Golden Boy. Somebody get me Temptation on the line, quick!" So the seed was planted—a little stolen water was better than no drink at all. Temptation is not an advocate of self-denial. He will always say something is better than nothing, and, at the same time, hide the consequences of that little bit of "something" behind his back.

No way is Temptation going to let you in on the fact that a secret sin on earth is an open scandal in heaven. Why, if you ever got a picture of the angels—eyebrows to scalp, jaws dropped to their chests, clutching their heavenly pearls— while God shakes His head in quiet disappointment, you would think twice about sneaking your hand into that cookie jar of sin, wouldn't you? But David found out soon enough— after the death of Uriah had been carried out, per his orders—

that even though God loved him, his disobedience would not be tolerated.

Eeny, Meeny, Miny, Moe

"How can a God of love be so cruel?" the world wonders while preachers scream, "Repent or suffer the consequences!" But there's nothing cruel about it. Each person chooses his own fate. No one gets angry when a contestant misses out on the grand prize because he chose the wrong door on *Let's Make a Deal*. We think, "Oh, well, tough luck. I had a feeling you should have chosen differently." No one gets angry at the host of the show or calls him cruel. Yet when it comes to people selecting their own destiny—when they've been given clear guidelines describing their options—God gets blamed for other people's bad choices. How? Why? At least God gives you the benefit of knowing what's behind each door.

Just as hell was never prepared for people but for Satan and his cohorts, God did not sit up in heaven plotting out and dreaming up the consequence for every sin, eagerly waiting to dish out the punishments. He doesn't have to. The laws of sowing and reaping work without His assistance. It was never His desire for us to suffer at all. The choice is up to each one of us. We get to choose the quality of our existence before God each and every day, just as we get to choose our eternity. God wants us to live life to the fullest, experiencing the kingdom of God right here on earth—righteousness, peace, and joy in the Holy Ghost. And that comes only through being obedient to His Word.

Another ploy of Temptation is to get you to believe that once you repent, God will feel sorry for you, eliminate the consequences, and clean up your mess for you. Not true! Yes, He will forgive you, but because His very nature is one of holiness, He has a standard that must be maintained. He is not a modern-day parent who allows His children to make Him look ridiculous in public. You know the type I'm talking about. The ones whose children throw those horrible, screaming tantrums in the middle of grocery stores and malls all over the world. You may have even been on the receiving end of this type of trauma, attempting to ignore the stares of others who wonder why you can't control your child.

Well, God will have no part of that. He will not circumvent the law of nature or spiritual order. He tells us no because He knows the outcome and wants us to avoid the pain of it. He chastens those whom He loves (see Hebrews 12:6). He realizes this is not a pleasant thing, but He is keeping His eye on the end benefit: "No discipline seems pleasant at the time, but painful. Later on, however, it produces a harvest of righteousness and peace for those who have been trained by it" (Hebrews 12:11 NIV). And so, with this in mind, He sent Nathan to call David on the carpet and deliver some very sobering words. First, Nathan let his highness know that his sin had not gone unnoticed. Second, he pronounced the judgment of God and the consequence of David's sin.

I believe David was actually relieved. I'm sure that after the headiness of the romance had worn off in the face of the immense responsibility that followed, David's heart had become heavy. What song could he sing to God after the mess he had made? Finally back to himself, he realized his indulgence was a direct sin against God Himself. This was the burden of his heart, even though he hadn't been caught redhanded. Whatever God decided to do was fair, as far as David was concerned. And in the light of such earnestness, God forgave David. He kept his status as a man after God's heart, but the consequences remained to haunt him forever— the death of the child Bathsheba carried. And because of the breach of godly example before his family, rebellion, betrayal, and embarrassing scandal took root in his own home, among his own children.

I'm sure these things were worse than death to David. I would venture to say that Temptation was getting a good chuckle out of the whole thing until he saw the fruit that was born out of what he thought was sure to be a disaster. Solomon, David and Bathsheba's "love child"—the second of four sons she bore to David after the death of their first son— went on to build the temple and become, next to his father, Israel's most widely respected king until Temptation got the best of him, too. This, however, did not erase Solomon's name from the ancestral lineage of Jesus Christ. It was just a temporary setback that took the joy out of his latter years. Oh, well, like father, like son. The struggle to remain standing continues.

6

WHERE BLIND MEN FALL

"Let no man say when he is tempted, I am tempted
of God: for God cannot be tempted with evil, neither tempteth he any man."

JAMES 1:13 KJV

TALK ABOUT THE SWING OF THE PENDULUM! As much as David
was a man after God's own heart, Saul was a man after his
own desires, as well as an unwitting victim of the whims of
the people. Strikingly handsome, impressive, a head taller
than any of the others—among the Israelites, he had no
equal. Though he had all the outward qualifications that made
him a prime candidate for kingship, his inner makeup left a
lot to be desired. I think it's safe to say that Saul was a king
without a clue. The poor guy never knew what hit him. Can
you imagine? One day you go out looking for your father's
lost donkeys, and the next thing you know you've been
anointed king. Now what do you do? Don't worry, Temptation will always be happy to give you a few suggestions.

Perhaps Saul knew he was God's reluctant answer to the people's demand for a king. Perhaps that gave him a complex and always kept him slightly off-kilter. Like an unwanted child who constantly battles with the demon of rejection, Saul sought to please the people...to his own demise. He lost sight of who was the ultimate power in order to exhibit his own, and he suffered a rude awakening—God was not impressed.

Too busy doing his own personal public relations, he forgot that—though he was king—he was required to answer to a higher authority. Saul was the epitome of a paradox. Though he was the tallest among his peers, he came from the smallest clan in Israel. Though he was a man of battle, he feared the opinions and reactions of the people. Though he had no problem lifting sacrifices to the Lord, he was repeatedly disobedient. Though determinedly vindictive, he could be equally repentant when confronted by David as to why he sought his life. What was the root of all of this inconsistency? Saul never understood that *God* was the source of all that he possessed. Robbing him of that knowledge was a meticulous job on the part of Temptation to destroy not just a man, but a nation. Temptation was too familiar with the Scripture that says, "Smite the shepherd and the sheep [of the flock] will be scattered" (Zechariah 13:7 AMP). The latter part of his agenda failed, but I believe Temptation had a good time viewing his handiwork in the life of Saul.

The Root of the Problem

So the people wanted a king. The prophet Samuel—who anointed Saul to be king—was upset, and God was upset. Both Samuel and God were insulted by the request of the people. How could they want a king when they already had the best King on earth, or in heaven, for that matter? But *nooo,* they wanted to be like all the other nations. They wanted a king who could be seen with the human eye. They felt a little weird relying on pillars of fire by night, clouds that moved by day, and earthquakes and such. A tall, handsome warrior would definitely be more politically correct. Was it the Kinks who sang, "Give the People What They Want"? Anyway, after warning the Israelites of the consequences of putting their lives and their welfare into the hands of a finite being, God decided they should find out the hard way that electing a human king was not the answer for a happy existence.

However, even up to the present day, royalty has always held a strange intrigue to the masses. Perhaps it's that worship thing. Because mankind was created to worship God, it stands to reason that a problem is created when they choose not to worship Him. The worship void remains empty. This results in man looking for something or someone to worship. Suddenly, ordinary people become demigods because of a simple title placed in front of their names. Just think—they don't sing beautifully, they don't perform amazing athletic feats on the basketball court, they've made no significant discoveries in science or medicine. They simply are *royalty*— glamorous, wealthy, *royalty*.

So God gave the people Saul, and they were pleased. He led them fearlessly against the Ammonites and won their admiration. At last they were like all the other nations; they had a king. Sad to say, they were about to discover you can never judge a book by its cover. Though he stood a head taller than everyone else on the outside, he was a small man inside because he lacked wisdom. And the lack of wisdom is a broad gateway to insecurity. Insecurity causes people to flail in the waters of life, which causes them to drown even faster, taking with them all who go along for the ride or try to rescue them.

Even on the day of his "ordination" it was obvious that Saul wasn't quite up to the job that was laid out for him. Here were all the tribes of Israel gathered for this momentous occasion, and Saul had hidden himself among the baggage. Small wonder some were heard to utter, "How can this fellow save us?" (1 Samuel 10:27 NIV). After all the Israelites had been through as a nation, they still didn't get it. Victory could only be achieved by the Spirit of God. So although Samuel explained to Saul that God would remain the ultimate power in Israel, Saul still developed a bad habit of taking matters into his own hands. Now, what could make a man who knew he didn't have what it takes to lead a nation to victory become so presumptuous? Could it be...Temptation?

The Right Soil for Disaster

Temptation loves Insecurity with its fertile, rich soil that's perfect for all of his horrible little schemes. Why, you can literally plant any kind of seed in Insecurity's vulnerable soil and watch a plant sprout up overnight. The right thought dropped here, the right little whisper placed there, and *voilà!* A nice little crop of sin flourishes like a patch of weeds in no time. Let's see, what do we have growing over here? Manipulation, embezzlement, lying, rebellion, jealousy, strife, even murder?! And all of this sprouted out of one little seed? *What is the name of that plant?* you might wonder. It's the plant of Ambition. It grows fastest when fertilized with a good dose of Greed, Fear, and Pride. Water that with a lust for Power, and you've got an obnoxious, uncontrollable crop on your hands with shoots sprouting in every direction.

Ever been to a concert or event and tried to get backstage afterward? If you have, we've probably shared a similar experience. The security guard is usually unreasonably surly, even to those who might actually have legal entry back into the hallowed territory of the greenroom. Why? Generally because this is the poor security guard's one big moment for power. He has been given the position of the gatekeeper and, by all means, no one is going in unless he says so.

I remember that after one especially unpleasant encounter with one of these sentries, I heard someone snidely remark, "His wife probably beats him when he gets home, so I guess this is all the power he gets to exert." Sad to say, there was probably a grain of truth in that statement. Temptation knows that Insecurity can work in his favor no matter which way the pendulum swings. It can completely paralyze its victim and render him ineffective. Or it can cause the victim to over-compensate by making rash decisions that usually sabotage his best intentions, thereby actually robbing him of the control he was seeking in the first place. Call it a Napoleonic complex, if you will. I say it was put in place by Temptation long before that famous French monarch came on the scene.

What the People Say

When it came to Saul, Temptation had already done his homework. Actually, this assignment was probably a no-brainer for him; he knew that Saul was completely clueless without the assistance of the Holy Spirit. And that meant he would always be a little jumpy, a little testy, a tad too impatient for his own good. This would definitely work to Temptation's benefit in the years to come. Also, though Saul had been God's choice for king, he knew that what Saul really longed for was to be the people's choice. It's that new-kid-on-the-block syndrome. The new kid either becomes the bully or the victim of the bully. "The people" can get you in a whole lot of trouble, but this seemed to be a lesson that Saul just couldn't learn. So Samuel would tell Saul what *God* wanted, and then Saul would do what the *people* wanted instead. How long did he think God would put up with that nonsense? Did he fancy himself indispensable? Or was God supposed to understand and acquiesce to Saul's point of view?

In 1 Samuel chapter 13, we find Saul preparing for battle. Seven days had passed as he waited for Samuel to come offer sacrifices to the Lord and bless the troops for victory. As the clock ticked past the designated time for Samuel's arrival, the natives began to get restless. They grumbled, they mumbled, they began to scatter. Enter Temptation, stage left; Impatience and Pressure, stage right. Poor Saul found himself center stage in a tight squeeze, pressed between the suggestions of his three hateful advisors. "What are you waiting for, the Philistines to come and eat you for lunch? Why not just hand them the silverware and napkins?" one sneered. "What do you think the people are going to say if you blow this one? You know you'll be the fall guy," another whispered. "Who needs Samuel anyway? After all, you're the king," hissed yet another. And with that, Saul puffed out his chest and said, "Yeah, that's right....I'm the man. I'm running this." And he promptly blew it.

Temptation giggled with glee. This assignment had been almost too simple for him. Impatience and Pressure were two of his favorite cohorts and, when mixed together, they were like a Molotov cocktail—one good shake and the victim was sure to explode and make a mess of things.

Just as Saul finished presenting a burnt offering to God, Samuel arrived. "What have you done?" he cried. And Saul's response? "Well, see, I thought...well, you know, I just felt led to present this burnt offering..."

When I was a little girl and took matters into my own hands, my excuse would always be, "Well, I thought..." My mother would always interrupt, "You know what thought made a man do?" I won't say what my mother told me here, but the result of his presumption was quite embarrassing. I think it would suffice to say that Saul's thoughts didn't exactly get him the response he was looking for. Samuel didn't care what Saul thought. Neither did God. "'You acted foolishly,' Samuel said. 'You have not kept the command the LORD your God gave you; if you had, he would have established your kingdom over Israel for all time. But now your kingdom will not endure; the LORD has sought out a man after his own heart and appointed him leader of his people, because you have not kept the LORD's command'" (1 Samuel 13:13-14 NIV). "Ah, yes, phase one accomplished," Temptation breathed.

Where Credit Is Due

Insecurity and impatience had caused Saul to ignore the voice of God quietly saying, "My dear child, don't you know, in patience you possess your soul" (see Luke 21:19). But Saul wasn't interested in possessing his soul. It was the *hearts of the people* he wanted to possess, even if it must cost him his own son. And so, with Temptation urging him on, Saul took the credit when his son Jonathan finally routed the Philistines, and refused to change an oath he impulsively uttered—an oath that could have cost Jonathan his life if the people hadn't refused to carry it out. All in the name of saving face. What a dad! Small wonder Jonathan ended up taking sides with David against his own father for the throne. Certainly there was no love lost between them!

Oh! But it doesn't end there. Saul continued his quest for power without event and won many victories for a while until the Lord sent him to conquer the Amalekites. And here Temptation made a smart move. Temptation likes to lull his victims into thinking they are being blessed because they have God's approval. *Maaajor* deception! Therefore, victims of Temptation never correct their attitudes or their actions. They continue on in the same frame of mind as before, with no situation presenting itself to make their mistake glaringly evident. They are walking tragedies just waiting to happen.

Temptation counts on us being consistent with our former behavior so that he can perpetrate his agenda of aborting our God-ordained destiny. God, too, bides His time in the interest of completing His purposes. He will keep us in the mix for as long as possible until our presence becomes a hindrance to maintaining the integrity of the recipe. At that point, He will call a time-out to reveal to us where we really live and remove us from the kitchen. No one ruins God's sauce, okay?

Again, Samuel gave Saul God's specific instructions: "Now go, attack the Amalekites and totally destroy everything that belongs to them. Do not spare them; put to death men and women, children and infants, cattle and sheep, camels and donkeys" (1 Samuel 15:3 NIV). But Saul got that thinking disease again. With a little assistance from Temptation, of course. Temptation's always so persuasive: "Now did the Lord *really* mean for you to kill King Agag? He actually doesn't fit into the mere man category. It would look so much more impressive to the people if you at least brought back the king as a captive, don't you think? And what about all those fat calves and lambs? What a waste! Why not keep them and sacrifice them to the Lord? He would certainly like that!" Temptation's reasoning sounded good to Saul, so off he went.

Now, the Bible says in 1 Samuel 15:9 that "Saul and the army spared Agag and the best of the sheep and cattle, the fat calves and lambs—everything that was good. These they were *unwilling* to destroy completely, but everything that was despised and weak they totally destroyed" (NIV, emphasis added). It's always easier to part with the stuff that doesn't really matter, isn't it? It's when God starts asking for the things that have wrapped themselves around our hearts that the power struggle truly begins. We find all kinds of justifications and excuses to delay the inevitable. So while Saul was doing his own thing once again—and feeling perfectly justified, mind you—the Lord had a talk with Samuel. In short, He said, "That's it, I've had it with Saul. Cut! Let's call it a wrap."

Feeling very distressed, poor Samuel was sent to deliver the news—only to find that not only had Saul been blatantly disobedient, he'd had a monument erected to his own honor. By the time Samuel caught up with Saul, I'm sure he was not in the best of humor. The king, however, was in a good mood, proudly proclaiming, "The LORD bless you! I have carried out the LORD's instructions" (1 Samuel 15:13). He actually believed he had done God's work. Temptation did a fine job of justifying Saul's disobedience and glossing over the fact that he had proceeded with his own agenda instead of God's. I can imagine the look on Samuel's face as he asked Saul, "What then is this bleating of sheep in my ears? What is this lowing of cattle that I hear?" (1 Samuel 15:14 NIV). In other words, "If you carried out the Lord's orders to kill everything moving, it's awfully noisy around here!"

The Deception of Denial

"Well, you see, it was the *soldiers* who brought them from the Amalekites," Saul said. "They spared the best of the sheep and cattle to sacrifice to the Lord your God, but don't worry. We totally destroyed the rest. Hey, you know I know how to follow orders…"

"Stop it!" cried an exasperated Samuel. "God said you disobeyed Him. Why?"

Temptation had done such a good snow job on Saul that he had the nerve to argue with a prophet of God. He believed in his heart of hearts that he was right! "But I *did* obey the Lord!" he said. "I went on the mission the Lord assigned me. I completely destroyed the Amalekites and brought back Agag, their king." (Wasn't the king an Amalekite too? I don't get it!) "It was those soldiers; *they* were the ones who took the sheep and the cattle from the plunder—the best of what was devoted to God—in order to sacrifice them to the Lord *your* God." (See 1 Samuel 15:15-21 to read this conversation in its entirety.)

I find a couple of things interesting here. The Bible states that *"Saul and the army* spared Agag and the best of the sheep and cattle" (1 Samuel 15:9 NIV, emphasis added). But later Saul says that it was the *soldiers* who did the dirty work. And what's this "the LORD *your* God" business (verse 21)? Wasn't He Saul's God, too? God can't do anything for us if we don't claim responsibility for our actions. Temptation knows his legal rights in this area well. That's why he gives Denial a lot of freelance work. When all other demons fail, Denial always delivers. Denial works closely with Shifting Blame. What a team! "It was that woman you gave me!" Remember the famous line that came rolling off Adam's lips when God questioned him about his strange behavior? Same *modus operandi,* different circumstances, but the "I was just an unwitting victim of the circumstances" line is always worth a try. Only thing is, this rationale never seems to work with God.

Samuel sums it up nicely: "Does the LORD delight in burnt offerings and sacrifices as much as in obeying the voice of the LORD? To obey is better than sacrifice, and to heed is better than the fat of rams. For rebellion is like the sin of divination, and arrogance like the evil of idolatry. Because you have rejected the word of the LORD, he has rejected you as king" (1 Samuel 15:22-23 NIV). The end, by God—short and sweet. You can almost hear Temptation saying, "Yesss! That was easy enough! What a sucker!"

They say confession is good for the soul, but when it comes too late, or if you simply confess because you've been caught in broad daylight, confession takes on the dull glow of brass trying to pass as gold. It just doesn't have the same brilliance. Poor Saul gave too little, too late. "You're right," he

finally confessed, "I have sinned. [No kidding!] I violated the
LORD's command and your instructions. I was afraid of the
people [I knew he would fit *them* in somewhere], and so I
gave in to them. Now I beg you, forgive my sin and come
back with me, so that I may worship the LORD" (1 Samuel
15:24-25 NIV). First of all, it wasn't Samuel's forgiveness that
Saul needed. Second, Samuel didn't want to be bothered; he
was finished. Besides, he knew that "godly sorrow brings
repentance that leads to salvation and leaves no regret, but
worldly sorrow brings death" (2 Corinthians 7:10 NIV). You
know the kind of worldly sorrow Paul was talking about in
this passage. The kind that keeps saying, "I'm sorry" and then
doing the same thing over and over again. Samuel recognized
exactly what Saul was doing. He knew that confession was
not enough. Repentance was needed. Confession for confession's sake is merely admission. God wants more than admission; He wants true confession. That is when we, first, agree
with what God thinks about what we did, and second,
resolve not to do it again. Now that is true repentance.

Saul had not yet arrived at this point. Samuel wanted no
part of whatever else Saul was involved in and told him so:
"Obviously, you didn't know who you were dealing with. But
now perhaps you've learned that God means what He says.
He's not some mere mortal who changes His mind to suit
other people's agendas. Get real!" (At least, that's how I think
Samuel would have said it if he were alive today.) So Samuel
killed the Amalekite king and retired to his house. He never
went to see Saul again.

Poor Saul! Reduced to living in even greater fear without
the reassurance of God's presence and protection, he sank
even deeper into depression—a depression that bordered on
insanity. But even this leftover morsel could be used in
Temptation's plan. In fact, it could be rather convenient. Why
not use Saul to wipe out the next up-and-coming king? The

buzz in the heavenly realms was that this king-to-be was really a man after God's own heart. If Temptation could get God's choice for king out of the way, it would kill two birds with one stone—it would be a really great jab at God *and* it would win him fabulous brownie points with his boss, Satan. But here, God made a divine executive decision and overrode Temptation's agenda with His own. David would sit on the throne, and Temptation would have to wait until another day to deal with him, in another arena.

Blind Ambition

This sad tale happens to countless others. The climb to the top is accomplished at breathtaking speed, but with not enough experience or character development obtained to secure a sound foundation for the person to stand on. Temptation makes sure these people forget where they came from and who was the source of their promotion. In these situations, Temptation makes sure the gift is beautifully polished in order to distract and blind them to the One who should remain their constant focus. Why else would Saul, who had the privilege of hearing directly from God, end up disguising himself so that he could seek the help of a psychic for advice? (Read 1 Samuel chapter 28 for that story.) This holds shades of modern-day activity!

Psychic hotlines have become one of America's favorite pastimes. Everybody wants to hear a good word. Everybody is curious about what's going to happen to them. Yet most people aren't asking God, who gives this information for free. They'd rather run up their phone bill on the hotlines or pay to visit a psychic in person. That way they're not held accountable for their actions. It's just like Saul wanting to be king of his own destiny. And so in the end he was—dying a solitary, self-inflicted death without honor.

Saul forgot that God was the One who put him at the top. He allowed Temptation to convince him that he was indispensable, and he refused to deal with his own flaws. He chose to listen to the roar of the people instead of the still, small voice of God. He literally threw away his destiny by trying to grasp it too tightly with his own hands. Like a bar of wet soap, the monarchy slipped through Saul's fingers as he leaned away from God's lordship to follow Temptation's suggestions.

Temptation will always give you a good reason to disobey God. He will always justify your inner longings. He will always make you believe your own press, then be the first to kick you to the curb once you lose your popularity, and remind you of all the embarrassing things you've done to get where you are. Yes, he'll lure you to the precipice of destruction, push you over the edge, and leave you in the arms of Condemnation to finish you off. And you won't even know what hit you because his smile is blinding.

While many in the church frown disapprovingly at secular entertainers whose acts have grown more and more outrageous in order to appeal to the masses, such finger-pointing is actually hypocritical. The church is not free of guilt in this same respect. Like Aaron, Moses' brother, many a pastor has been a people-pleaser. Many a pastor has helped his congregation build a golden calf. Many a pastor has yielded to the mandates of the church board or congregation when he or she received specific instructions from God to take the church in a new direction or preach a more convicting sermon. Resistance has caused many pastors to compromise their decisions and the message of the cross. Why? Because Temptation stands nearby, cautioning them, "If you preach that, the people will leave and take their tithes with them. Then what will you do? You know the board will say it's your fault and boot you out. That's all the thanks you'll get for teaching that holiness mess." And so the pastor determines that it's best not to rock the boat. After all, if it ain't broke, why fix it?

Of course, another important point—one that becomes clear in our study of Saul—is that if Temptation can't draw you into complete disobedience, he will simply pervert your worship. He will get you to go through all the motions while your heart is far removed from God. Those who have dealt with an unfaithful mate have voiced the sentiment, "Your body's here with me, but your mind is somewhere else." I think some of us are like that with God. I always wonder: Do these people really believe they're actually fooling God? Temptation knows that the quickest way for you to disappoint God is to "play church." You need to know that if Temptation can't beat you, he'll join you and influence you to become "religious" and appearance-driven. He will get you so focused on the outer that your "good works" will become rote actions, while your heart lies dormant, no longer stirred by the things of God. That's about as lukewarm as you can get. And you know what happens to the lukewarm? God spews them out of His mouth (see Revelation 3:16). That's a sad end for someone who starts off so illustrious in the things of God.

And so it is for all who get convenient amnesia once they reach their goals and acquire wealth, position, and fame, forgetting where they came from and who promoted and elevated them. For all who reach the top and leave God behind, victory becomes empty. Like the caterpillar who reached the top in the wonderful book *Hope for the Flowers,* the horrified whispers of "there's nothing up here" will resound through their souls and leave them as disillusioned as Solomon, who summed up life sighing, "All is vanity" (Ecclesiastes 1:2 KJV). The end is always the same: "For what will it profit a man if he gains the whole world, and loses his own soul?" (Mark 8:36 NKJV). But Temptation won't tell you that.

"All we like sheep have gone astray; we have turned, every one, to his own way" (Isaiah 53:6 NKJV). Sheep have been known to eat their way off a cliff. Poor things, they just didn't know. They never looked up; they were too busy feeding on their own needs. Temptation is the master of focusing our attention on our needs. And we, like sheep, go straight over the edge every time we choose to linger too long and nibble on the things that feed our flesh. As long as we're focused on ourselves, Temptation will be there to drop yet another crumb on the path that leads us closer to our destruction, whereas one look up could change the course of history.

7

BEAUTY AND THE BEAST

"Be ye doers of the word, and not hearers only, deceiving your own selves."

JAMES 1:22 KJV

SOMEONE ONCE SAID THAT WHEN you walk in the dark you will stumble and fall, and when you walk in the light you will also stumble and fall. The only difference is, you will be able to see what you're tripping over. On one end of the spectrum we have Saul caught up in a torrid and disastrous affair with Temptation, all because of his failure to heed the word of the Lord and make wise choices. But Solomon—now there's a different story! What was his excuse? How did a man who was renowned for his wisdom end his life in such a state of disillusionment?

Solomon started off well enough. His father, David, left him with the best instructions anyone could give: "I am about to go the way of all the earth....So be strong, show yourself a man, and observe what the LORD your God requires: Walk in his ways, and keep his decrees and commands, his laws and requirements, as written in the Law of Moses, so that you may prosper in all you do and wherever you go, and that the LORD may keep his promise to me…" (1 Kings 2:2-4 NIV). He went on to say something prophetic: "You are a man of wisdom" (verse 9 NIV). And so he was. When God told Solomon to ask for whatever he wanted from Him, Solomon made a very wise choice. He asked for wisdom, wishing for a discerning heart to govern the people and distinguish between right and wrong.

Here, Temptation began to rub his chin. *Hmm, this might prove to be a bit more challenging than expected,* he thought. He could no longer count on Solomon's youth and inexperience. He was going to have to reach back into the gene pool and see what he could scrounge up there. Let's see…an exaggerated weakness for women! That was always a good one. The lust of the flesh could always be counted on when all else failed. Temptation had legal grounds to use this nugget because God visits "the iniquity of the fathers upon the children unto the third and fourth generation" (Exodus 20:5 KJV). We'll discuss this in a later chapter, but for now let's see if sonny-boy will follow in the tradition of his father and fall for the same old trick. It'll be interesting to see if he's made of stronger stock.

"Hmm," mused Temptation, "let's see what else we might have here…*voilà!* Solomon didn't ask for a mind to *do* what was right. He merely asked for wisdom, and that doesn't mean he has to use it. Even smart people can have lapses and do stupid things, so it's simply a matter of time for Solomon. Perhaps I should give Compromise a call. This might be a good assignment for him." Temptation rubbed his hands together; he was really warming to the idea of tempting his new subject. There was an art to this thing, you know. Hmm…Deception would fit nicely into this plan. Oh, this was going to be good!

Looks Can Be Deceiving

As children we grew up hearing the story about the ugly duckling, who turned into a beautiful swan, or we were told about the beast, who was actually a handsome prince who'd had a spell cast on him. Real life, however, usually paints such scenarios the other way around. Things, situations, and people in our lives usually start off looking too good to be true, and they usually are. And we have ample warning of these things. "Even Satan can disguise himself as an angel of light" (2 Corinthians 11:14 NLT). The most attractive opportunities have turned into hideous nightmares for people who didn't take the time to investigate exactly what they were getting into. These "wonderful" opportunities usually come cloaked in urgency. We are all familiar with those "for a limited time only" offers. Jump on it now, find out it's a bad idea later. We get sucked in almost every time because the root of our problem is a basic lack of trust in God's provision.

Why Solomon felt he had to help God in securing peace for Israel is beyond me. God had done a good job of making Israel a secure nation—one that was feared by other nations—before Solomon took over. Funny how we do that. We seem to forget that God has been doing His job for a long time and He knows how to do it quite well without any help from us, thank you very much. Yet Solomon felt the need to marry foreign women in order to secure his political alliances. Or so went his rationale. And so each of his lovely wives came dragging her own gods behind her. And, for the sake of keeping the peace, Solomon had to indulge them, accommodate them, and eventually participate in their little visits to the high places for worship.

It's been said that if you choose to marry an unbeliever, you get the devil for a father-in-law and—with all due respect for your spouse—you cannot get rid of him. The Bible says it more succinctly: "Can a man take fire in his bosom, and his clothes not be burned?" (Proverbs 6:27 KJV). What is it that makes teenagers blind to the fact that, no matter how many times they sneak around and violate their parents' rules, they always get caught? They're caught by the consequences, as well as by those who laid down the law.

The warning is clear enough: "Do not merely listen to the word, and so deceive yourselves. Do what it says. Anyone who listens to the word but does not do what it says is like a man who looks at his face in the mirror and, after looking at himself, goes away and immediately forgets what he looks like. But the man who looks intently into the perfect law that gives freedom, and continues to do this, not forgetting what he has heard, but doing it—he will be blessed in what he does" (James 1:22-25 NIV). The opposite of that, my friend, is you will not be blessed. As a matter of fact, because we are told by God that we have the option to choose life or death and blessings or curses (see Deuteronomy 30:19), we're not left with much gray area should we choose to violate His Word. The consequences are clear.

Yet, in spite of David's specific instructions, Solomon violated God's law. Not only did he add wives to himself, he added *foreign* wives. Not only did he add foreign wives to himself, he added *a lot of them*—seven hundred, to be exact! Plus three hundred concubines! That made one thousand beautiful, exotic women, all luring Solomon in one thousand different directions, farther and farther away from God. Let's face it, I doubt he even noticed the glory of God fading in the distance as he became surrounded by all those batting eyelashes and that thick haze of perfume.

Sex, Lies, and Compromise

Certainly men and women are no different today in their fascination with each other. How many times have we seen some good Christian man or woman going through hardship to maintain a relationship with an unbeliever? No amount of sound counsel from concerned friends and family can convince the Christian that this relationship is detrimental to their walk with God. In other words, it's not conducive to maintaining holiness. Temptation knows that once he gets you in the grip of the world, it's hard to free yourself from its hold. Like a python, the allure of the world is downright hypnotic, paralyzing you from having good judgment. And there you are, feeling warm and cozy, until you realize the life is slowly being squeezed out of you. Then it's too late. The world doesn't let go easily, and neither does condemnation.

It's not the nonthreatening, ineffective Christians who get hit. It's the ones who have inspired others to give their hearts to Jesus, and who live holy lives sold out to prayer and sanctification. These are the ones Temptation goes after—the man or woman with a mind made up to serve the Lord uncompromisingly. The struggle to regain your footing can be a long and arduous process. Meanwhile, others are affected negatively in the body of believers. And you know the rest: "A little leaven leavens the whole lump" (1 Corinthians 5:6 NKJV).

How many of us have thrown up our hands in despair when the people we looked up to came crashing down from their pedestals, tarnished and worse for the wear? Temptation is always right there to add salt to the wound by rubbing in the salve of Self-pity and Doubt. *Well, if they couldn't maintain a standard, how can I?* we think.

Perhaps this is why Paul, after making a clear case for not being unequally yoked with unbelievers, then includes wayward believers into the same category of undesirable company. He advises, "I am writing to you that you must not associate with anyone who calls himself a brother but is sexually immoral or greedy, an idolater or a slanderer, a drunkard or a swindler. With such a man do not even eat"

(1 Corinthians 5:11 NIV). Why, Paul? Because sin is strangely contagious. It's like when you go for a swim on a cold day. You stick your toe in first, but conviction hits you, and you recoil from the cold. Then you put your foot in and begin to gradually get used to the temperature. Slowly, ever so slowly, you begin to warm up and, next thing you know, you're all the way in, completely wet and feeling no pain, floating away on the current. At that point it's become easier to float than to swim back to shore. Attempting to swim back would require too much exertion. Plus, the minute you come out of the water, you're going to feel the cold even more bitterly than before. No, it's better to stay in, plus, now it feels so good!

So Temptation isn't pushy. He knows it works better if the sin is your idea. He merely dangles the worm that causes you to go for the bait—hook, line, and sinker.

Solomon went for Temptation's bait big time. He started with an Egyptian princess, and the rest is history. Nehemiah uses him as an example to warn the Israelites against marrying foreigners: "Was it not because of marriages like these that Solomon king of Israel sinned? Among the many nations there was no king like him. He was loved by his God, and God made him king over all Israel, but even he was led into sin by foreign women" (Nehemiah 13:26 NIV). Now to those who married and *then* came to the Lord—yet their spouses are still unbelievers—I believe that God extends special grace. But those who choose unbelieving partners after acquiring the knowledge of Christ must do some self-examination. "Can two walk together unless they are agreed?" (Amos 3:3 NKJV). Another translation says, "...unless they had met?" In other words, unless they had a meeting of the minds? A meeting of the minds concerning what? Try this one on for size: "What do righteousness and wickedness have in common? Or what fellowship can light have with darkness? What harmony is there between Christ and Belial? What does a believer have in common with an unbeliever?" (2 Corinthians 6:14-15 NIV). How deep is your love for God? How important is His approval to You? What is more important: your desire, or His perfect will for your life? We can all rationalize making concessions especially in the area of "love." But is your choice something that God can approve and bless?

Solomon's reasoning that marriage was a surefire way to secure major political alliances was flawed but correct. After all, what father would attack the country where his daughter lived? The flip side of this whole arrangement was that these foreign women were downright beautiful. Therefore, it wasn't exactly a sacrifice Solomon made on behalf of his country. But in the end, it cost him more than he gained. He was led away into idol worship.

I wonder why Solomon didn't realize that the anger of God is always to be feared far beyond man's displeasure. Perhaps he was too busy doing what many of us are guilty of doing—intellectualizing, thinking that God needs our help to secure what He has so freely given us. Whatever we think while we're caught up in the rationalizations of compromise, it behooves us to remember that those who seek to be friendly with the world have chosen to be an "enemy of God" (see James 4:4 NIV). And that is a needless expense because "when a man's ways please the LORD, He makes even his enemies to be at peace with him" (Proverbs 16:7 NKJV). Politics and compromise are bedfellows who usually awaken quite surprised to find out how little their rendezvous has accomplished. Their covert trysts have never quite led either party to where it wanted to go. And so it was with Solomon. He got sucked into the world and eventually lost sight of heaven in a fog of depression.

When the Love Bug Bites

Led into sin! How is one person led into sin by another? Jesus said, "If you love Me, keep My commandments" (John 14:15 NKJV). Love is what makes us rearrange our way of doing things. Love makes us want to do whatever it takes to make the object of our affection feel good about us and life in general. Jesus knew that "where your treasure is, there will your heart be also" (Matthew 6:21 KJV). Love will make you like things you never liked before. Remember the popular song that went, "If loving you is wrong, I don't wanna be right"? Think about that statement. What kind of nonsense is that? It makes no sense at all to the logical mind, but to the heart...now, that's another matter! What makes a man ditch his devoted wife, the children he loves so dearly, the house he worked so hard to build, and run off with his secretary? Love—or lust—will make people gamble with their lives and all they hold dear. Temptation knows how to hit where he's sure it will hurt.

The Bible says King Solomon loved many foreign women besides Pharaoh's daughter—Moabites, Ammonites, Edomites, Sidonians, and Hittites. They came from nations that the Lord had warned the Israelites about: "You must not intermarry with them, because they will surely turn your hearts after their gods" (1 Kings 11:2 NIV). How could he be happy worshiping silent idols after knowing a God who had spoken to him personally? Small wonder his sad story concludes: "I discovered that a seductive woman is more bitter than death. Her passion is a trap, and her soft hands will bind you. Those who please God will escape from her, but sinners will be caught in her snare. [Ladies, its safe to say this can also be said of seductive men.] This is my conclusion.... I came to this result after looking into the matter from every possible angle. Just one out of every thousand men I interviewed can be said to be upright, but not one woman!" (Ecclesiastes 7:26-28 NLT).

Sounded a little jaded and weary, didn't he? He should have been; he had interviewed a thousand women intimately in order to find this out.

The Works of Josephus is even harder on Solomon. The author states, "Solomon grew mad in his love of women, and laid no restraint on himself in his lusts; nor was he satisfied with the women of his country alone, but he married many wives of foreign nations...and he transgressed the laws of Moses, which forbade Jews to marry any but those that were of their own people. He also began to worship their gods, which he did in order to win the gratification of his wives, and out of his affection for them...."

Josephus, quite unforgiving of Solomon's total disregard for the law, cited, "Solomon was fallen headlong into unreasonable pleasures, and regarded not those admonitions (the law) for when he had married seven hundred wives, the daughters of princes, and of eminent persons, and three hundred concubines, and these besides the king of Egypt's daughter, he soon was governed by them, till he came to imitate their practices. He was forced to give them this demonstration of his kindness and affection to them, to live according to the laws of their countries. And as he grew into years, his reason became weaker by length of time, it was not sufficient to recall to mind the institutions of his own country; so he still more and more condemned his own God, and continued to regard the gods that his marriages had introduced." This was missionary dating at its finest. And it proves that it's the missionary who usually gets converted in such relationships. Once an intimate alliance is formed with an unbeliever, Temptation now has the believer exactly where he wants him—in line for a change of heart and mind.

Now, this plays out in two different ways, naturally and spiritually. Solomon was led away to worship the gods of his wives. Remember, "No one can serve two masters. Either he will hate the one and love the other, or he will be devoted to the one and despise the other" (Matthew 6:24). This was spiritual adultery of the highest order. But the gods took on different shapes and personas. Not only did Solomon find himself wallowing in a lustful free-for-all, he found himself caught up in something that could ultimately be more destructive. Appeasing one area of flesh only awakens other cravings. With so many women, he needed to build luxurious palaces and suites to accommodate them. He was obligated to lavish on them a sumptuous lifestyle, as well as set himself up in the proper manner appropriate for a king. That called for money, and lots of it. So taxes were increased.

Temptation was more than happy to assist in spreading the cancer throughout Solomon's system. "Well, you've done all right by God," Temptation hissed. "You deserve to indulge yourself now. After all, a man of your status and fame should have a fabulous palace. I mean, here you are with this reputation for having all this knowledge, with people coming from all over the world to hear what you have to say. You can't entertain them in a home that looks any old way. You've got to set it out. Put on the Ritz!

"And what about all those wives? You'd better set them up right or you're going to have a mess on your hands." And all of what Temptation said was perfectly true. In the end, it took Solomon longer to build his palace (twenty years) than it did to build the temple of the Lord (seven years). He increased forced labor in Israel just to complete the palace. Then, of course, he had to add thousands of horses and chariots to squire all of these people around. Mm hm, you got it. Solomon ended up doing all of the things God told him *not* to do. Though he started off with good intentions, Solomon was now officially out of control.

Call it the avalanche effect—the little rolling pebble picked up speed and claimed everything else lying in the way as it rolled on and on out of control. Eventually there was only one thing that could happen. It had to crash. "Vanity, vanity, all is vanity…" Solomon sighed in retrospect, as Temptation whispered, "Oh, don't despair! You must admit, sin *is* pleasurable…for a season" (see Hebrews 11:25).

The Danger of Good Intentions

And so it is with us, trying to keep up with the Joneses— or simply trying to keep up appearances. Good intentions cause many of us to descend into the sea of debt. Before we know it, the trappings we've acquired take on a life of their own. The nice clothes deserve a better car, the fabulous car deserves an artfully landscaped driveway with a drive-in garage, the garage deserves a nice house attached to it, the nice house deserves better furniture.…In the end, we see a frustrated husband working his fingers to the bone, looking into the angry face of his wife and the disappointed gazes of his children as they sing a unified chorus of, "You never have time for us." He stands wordless, thinking to himself, *I have been killing myself, working hard to give my family everything they want, and they're still not happy. What more do they want from me?*

Even in the ministry, good intentions become larger than the wallets of the dreamers. And so Temptation whispers, "Go ahead, take another offering. People need to learn how to give to the work of the Lord, anyway." And ministry gradually, without hint or warning, becomes a business. When someone eventually mentions that money-raising efforts are overshadowing ministry to the people, their comments are met defensively: "People in the world give money with utter abandon to causes less worthy than the gospel. Why are the people in the church so stingy?"

I'll venture to say that I believe it's because those "people in the world" give because they are consumed with passion over their chosen issue. Passion is missing from the church. Temptation has stolen it—stolen it and directed it elsewhere. Today, most people in the church—lay people and leaders alike—can be found singing a common chorus of, "What about what *I* want? What about what *I* need?"

Passion for the things of God and for His agenda was what brought the early church together to sell everything they had and have all things in common (see Acts 2:42-47 for the full account). The apostles spent their time in prayer, tapping into the power of God. Signs and wonders followed, and the people gave because they were consumed with passion for God—a God who showed Himself strong in their midst and who had proven He was worthy of all they had to give. It was the anointing of God that moved people to give to the work of furthering the gospel of Jesus Christ. They weren't moved by pleas for a hundred people to give a hundred dollars, second or third offerings, or letters in the mail that promised an anointing cloth for a donation. As long as the focus was on God, not man, the people gave.

"Well, even Solomon said money answers all things," Temptation whispers. "Christians! They're the only ones who always want something for nothing. They want to pull on the anointing and get a miracle for free! It's not fair! It takes money to build churches. It takes money to travel and spread the gospel. And what about you? Don't you deserve something for all your hard work? People just don't realize how much it takes to really serve God." And so many a minister has found himself playing on the emotions of the people, selling the promises of God for profit, or, like the sons of Eli, abusing their position and taking multiple offerings by force.

The Bible says that the sons of Eli were literally skimming off the top of the the peoples' offerings to the Lord: "They treated the LORD's offerings with contempt" (1 Samuel 2:17 NLT). Another translation says, "The people came to scorn the

Lord's sacrifices."[5] The people became unwilling to give, just like the present day. God was not pleased, and their end was a bitter one because they had disgraced the name of the Lord. It was because of the sons of Eli that the people, in anticipation of Eli's death, cried out for a king to rule Israel rather than submitting to his sons' corrupt leadership.

Pressing for offerings without the anointing is something that grieves the spirit of the people and becomes a blemish on God's reputation. The world delights in accusing the church of taking people's money. Perhaps it's Temptation who has caused some ministries to have eyes that are bigger than their stomachs. A program that God has not designed and ordained will not be covered with the grace it takes to gain the provision needed.

"But you don't understand!" Temptation wails. "This is such a good idea! Think of what it would accomplish for God." But was it God's idea, or your idea? Man-made ideas will always require man-made efforts to accomplish them. God-inspired, God-breathed inventions, however, set the stage for God to perform and deliver provision supernaturally. God has a way of taking care of His own. It always has been, and always will be, God's anointing that will break the yoke off of people's minds, hearts, and wallets. Anything else will be an arduous affair, only achieved by the sweat of one's brow, the grumbling of the multitudes, and the shadow of the smeared reputation of the cross. And still Temptation presses, "This is for God! This is to make Him look good! There couldn't possibly be anything wrong with that!" And we're off and running in a flurry of fund-raising activity, whether for the kingdom or for our own personal comfort. This is not to say that all fund-raising is out of order. But we must make sure that we are operating in accordance with God's agenda and not our own.

Yes, Solomon got carried away with his building pro-
grams, and everyone in the country had to pay for them.
The people were not amused. This set the stage for God and the
people to grow increasingly disgruntled with Solomon. The
end result? God's decision to tear the kingdom from the grasp
of Solomon's sons. Proverbs 29:2 says, "When the righteous
are in authority, the people rejoice: but when the wicked
beareth rule, the people mourn" (KJV).

Times haven't changed that drastically. When people are
deciding which politicians to elect, they still consider who is
in favor of raising taxes and who wants to lower them. I
wouldn't say that Solomon was a wicked king; he simply got
a little sidetracked in his agenda. Let's just say he got a little
bit of a push toward his fall from grace, courtesy of Temptation's allies Lust and Pride.

Pride Comes Before the Fall

Pride really knows how to set people up for the kill. He
will convince you that appearances must be kept up at all
costs. The roads leading into the capital city of Solomon's
kingdom had to be paved and covered with smooth black
tar. After all, first impressions were lasting ones. The palace
was designed to be resplendent so that guests would gasp in
awe and return to their respective countries with firsthand
reports on the excellence of Solomon's wisdom and splendor.

Wasn't this the same trick that, years later, set up Hezekiah
to be completely plundered by the Babylonians? Poor
Hezekiah, so proud of all he had accumulated, showed every
inch of his acquired goodies to the Babylonians: "There was
nothing in his palace or kingdom that Hezekiah did not show
them" (2 Kings 20:13 NLT). The Babylonians politely took
note and later returned to take all that they had seen and haul
it off to Babylon. What they didn't take they destroyed,
leaving the land desolate for seventy years.

In the movie *The Godfather*, the character of Don Corleone, played by Marlon Brando, cryptically suggests that one should "keep your friends close, and your enemies even closer." But the Bible suggests that one should not "tell your left hand what your right hand is doing" (Matthew 6:3 NLT). Although this Scripture refers to charitable acts, it is a piece of advice one is wise to heed. Some people will not always be happy about your blessings, especially if they themselves are less fortunate. There is a difference between a prideful show that attempts to elevate one's self in the eyes of other people and a sincere testimony of God's goodness for the sake of His glory. Temptation doesn't mind if you're not able to discern the difference. All the better to manipulate you, my dear....

8

THE SNARE OF THE SNAKE

"Because that, when they knew God, they glorified
him not as God, neither were thankful; but became
vain in their imaginations, and their foolish heart was
darkened. Professing themselves to be wise, they
became fools."

ROMANS 1:21-22 KJV

How QUICKLY WE FORGET THE REASON we are here! Merrily
we roll along on our own way, mapping out our own agenda
as the elders cry, "Thou art worthy, O Lord, to receive glory
and honor and power: for thou hast created all things, and for
thy pleasure they are and were created" (Revelation 4:11 KJV).
Somewhere along the way, most of us have become con-
fused. The fact that man was created for God's pleasure—to
bring *Him* glory by honoring and rendering power unto Him
through our express obedience—became lost in the shuffle
as we tried to acquire our own personal comfort zones.

We have changed the glory of God into a caricature of
Santa Claus as some quarters of religion promote a "name it,
claim it, and frame it" mentality. Following this line of reasoning, God should now be moved by our whims. He should

jump to our tune since we've chosen to bless Him with our presence in the kingdom. He owes us. Because we've chosen to acknowledge Him as Abba Father, He should by all means be an indulgent papa and spoil us rotten. "Ask and ye shall receive." Isn't that what Scripture says (see Matthew 7:7)? Yes, it does, but in 1 John 5:14 we find something added on: "If we ask anything *according to his will,* he heareth us" (KJV, emphasis added). Yeah, but now we get to debate what His will is for us individually. That's where things get very interesting. According to the justifications of the flesh, we often decide what God should want for us. But, as the saying goes, "What's good to ya, ain't always good for ya." That's what God knows, but it seems to take us a little while to figure that out.

Solomon found out and came to a sad conclusion: "I said to myself, 'Come now, let's give pleasure a try. Let's look for the "good things" in life.' But I found that this, too, was meaningless....While still seeking wisdom, I clutched at foolishness....Anything I wanted, I took. I did not restrain myself from any joy....But as I looked at everything I had worked so hard to accomplish, it was all so meaningless. It was like chasing the wind. There was nothing really worthwhile anywhere" (Ecclesiastes 2:1,3,10-11 NLT). Truly, those who seek to save their lives will lose them (see Matthew 16:25).

What a sad state of affairs. While God is seeking worshipers to worship the Father in spirit and in truth (see John 4:23-24), we are all busy seeking our own satisfaction, urged on by the hissing voice of Temptation: "You owe it to yourself! Tomorrow isn't promised, you know. You'd better stop and smell those roses, take a little piece of the pie for yourself now." Yes, instant gratification is the name of the game. Consciously—or perhaps unconsciously—we all get sucked into the vortex of self-seeking. Old habits are hard to break, even after we give our lives to Christ. Someone once said that the only problem with a living sacrifice is that it keeps crawling off the altar. It's that "little piece for yourself" that becomes the huge stumbling block we all trip over.

The Temptation of Satan

Satan himself was the first victim of "me-itis," the selfishness disease. Who tempted him? I would venture to say he grew drunk from God's indulgence. In Ezekiel chapter 28, God reflects on the turning away of Lucifer with the sorrow of a father viewing his child who has fallen and damaged himself irreparably, all by his own rebellious will. There is nothing sadder to behold than self-inflicted victimization. After Absalom's death, David, who had watched Absalom lead Israel in revolt against him, cried out, "O my son Absalom, my son, my son Absalom! would God I had died for thee, O Absalom, my son, my son!" (2 Samuel 18:33 KJV). One wonders how much of the blame a father takes when his children openly destroy themselves in the face of all advice.

God, also, reminisced about better days spent in relationship with Lucifer: "You were the perfection of wisdom and beauty. You were in Eden, the garden of God. Your clothing was adorned with every precious stone—red carnelian, chrysolite, white moonstone, beryl, onyx, jasper, sapphire, turquoise, and emerald—all beautifully crafted for you and set in the finest gold. They were given to you on the day you were created. I ordained and anointed you as the mighty angelic guardian. You had access to the holy mountain of God and walked among the stones of fire" (Ezekiel 28:12-14 NLT).

This passage conjures up images of spoiled brats the world over whose parents find themselves in a state of dismay as they watch their precious charges—who have never suffered from a lack of anything—totally turn against them in the name of independence. At the height of their rebellion, these children often spit out venomous accusations such as "You never loved me anyway."

"How could they say that?" the parents wonder. "We made sure we gave them everything. We never wanted them to go through what we went through as children." And it turns out that well-intentioned indulgence produced the opposite of what the parents had hoped for. Instead, their vow to give their children a better life birthed a total lack of character—with the end product being demanding, self-involved, petulant young men or women seething with anger, unable to put their finger on why they are so dissatisfied with life.

There is something about a struggle that produces the sweetest of fruits. It is in the piercing that the headiest perfume is released. It is in the crushing that the richest oils flow forth. Rewards fought for are always most appreciated. Even Jesus "learned obedience from the things he suffered" (Hebrews 5:8 NLT).

In the book of Ezekiel, God goes on to say, about Satan, "You were blameless in all you did from the day you were created" (28:15 NLT). But then something happened. "You were blameless...until the day evil was found in you" (28:15 NLT). How? How could this happen? I mean, really! Here you are, the most gorgeous thing in creation, quite literally. You have access to all three realms of the universe—the heavenlies, the holy mountain of God; the earth, the Garden of Eden; and beneath the earth, among the stones of fire. There you are, God's right-hand man, ordained to a high position, anointed by God Himself! You're leading the worship, collecting all the praise and taking it up to heaven. Everybody knows you are the man. You have the respect of all the other angelic hosts. Complete *carte blanche!* And then one day you decide it's not enough. What could you be thinking at a time like that? Well, God said of Lucifer, "Your heart was filled with pride because of all your beauty. You corrupted your wisdom for the sake of your splendor" (Ezekiel 28:17 NLT). Another translation states, "Your beauty made you arrogant, you misused your wisdom to increase your dignity."[6]

The Fall of an Angel

In other words, Lucifer started believing his own press. In his mind, if he were that awesome, why not take it all? Why should he stress himself out taking all the praises up to God? What kind of a chump did God take him for, anyway? If he was the one collecting the praises, he should just keep them. Why should he do all the work and God reap all the rewards? Let God get His own praises. In all this huge cosmos, there was definitely room for two of them. (He wasn't stupid enough to think he could replace or totally get rid of God.) He had earned the right to be looked up to as God. And so Lucifer proudly pronounced, "I will ascend into heaven, I will exalt my throne above the stars of God: I will sit *also* upon the mount of the congregation, in the sides of the north: I will ascend above the heights of the clouds; I will be *like* the most High" (Isaiah 14:13-14 KJV, emphasis added). Five "I wills." For each one, Christ took a blow that resounded, "No, you will not," as they nailed His two hands and His two feet to the cross and pierced Him in His side. The humility of Christ extinguished the pride of Satan.

Yes, Pride was on the prowl even way back then when Satan was on God's good side. His whisper filled Satan's heart with loathing for heavenly protocol. "Oh, enough of this good little choirboy routine. It's time you got a little of the action for yourself. What are you getting out of all of this? Go ahead—go for it! He's too busy to notice, anyway."

Big mistake! God did notice, and took note: "In the pride of your heart you say, 'I am a god....' But you are a man and not a god, though you think you are as wise as a god" (Ezekiel 28:2 NIV).

Not only did God take note, He went a step further, much to the surprise of Satan, I would guess. As many a spoiled child is shocked when his or her indulgent parents finally decide to cut the apron strings, I would dare say the punishment was not what Satan expected: "So I drove you in disgrace from the mount of God, and I expelled you, O guardian cherub, from among the fiery stones....I threw you to the earth....I made a fire come out from you, and it consumed you" (Ezekiel 28:16-18 NIV). On that note, Satan was brought down to earth along with his foolish cronies who had the audacity to follow him in his madness.

It's hard to imagine that one who got to taste such a perfect existence could be tempted to blow it all for a try at something "more," whatever that is. In this case, more became less than nothing. It's almost as if Satan voted to trade all of his accumulated prizes for the bonus behind the mystery curtain, only to have it reveal a booby prize. No wonder he is filled with so much hatred and vengefulness.

Isaiah shed light on the motives of Babylon when he prophesied, "How the oppressor has come to an end! How his fury has ended! The LORD has broken the rod of the wicked, the scepter of the rulers, which in anger struck down peoples with unceasing blows, and in fury subdued nations with relentless aggression" (Isaiah 14:4-6 NIV). This is the same motivation behind the fire that now consumes our adversary Satan. His anger and his fury are relentless. His enemy—God; his victims—mankind. His *modus operandi*— the very same thing that made him fall. If it worked on him, certainly it will entrap those who are much more limited in knowledge and spiritual breadth.

Satan learned too late that "God resists the proud, but gives grace to the humble" (James 4:6 NKJV). But now that he knows, that's just as good a place to start with us. And it has worked from the beginning of time, starting with Eve, trickling down to Cain and landing in our hearts. This is a struggle over our worship, whether it be in the form of obedience or giving. Satan's whole thing was about stealing worship from God, in any and every form. From tithes and offerings to our obedience, anything that was a tribute to God, Satan vowed to steal or corrupt. The pattern was always the same, though it appeared in different shades of gray. Attack the offering (the worship) through lust and selfishness, and, if that failed, inject pride into the heart of the unassuming victim.

The lust thing worked like a dream with Adam and Eve. Cain and Abel became Satan's next project. Abel slipped through the cracks, but he struck pay dirt with Cain—disobedience *and* murder. Wow! Talk about killing two birds with one stone! If the rest of the human race responded as easily, getting revenge against God was going to be a piece of cake! God tried to help Cain out by suggesting he get an attitude adjustment and resubmit his offering: "Why are you angry? Why is your face downcast? If you do what is right, will you not be accepted? But if you do not do what is right [worship Me properly with the right offering], sin is crouching at your door; it desires to have you, but you must master it" (Genesis 4:6-7 NIV).

What a revelation! Wrong worship invites sin. Sin hides behind the door, waiting for us to take our focus off of worshiping God and off of rendering all that we are and all that we have to Him. So sin waited for Cain to absolutely refuse to correct his offering unto God, thus giving leeway for sin to open the door and usher in Murder and Lies. Who did Cain think he was dealing with? After killing Abel, he had the nerve, when questioned by God on Abel's whereabouts, to say he didn't know where his brother was! We as human beings are truly extremists. We go from one end of the spectrum to the other, and seldom in between. One camp feels it is exempt from the wrath of God and He should bless our mess. The other is bent over in guilt and condemnation about every little thing they do. What a chess game! Those who choose to revel in the flesh become Satan's pawns, which he moves at his pleasure. Only those who choose to live crucified lives are in the position to declare, "Checkmate!"

The Eye of the Needle

Those who have, long for more, while those who don't have feel privileged to give. It is a well-known fact that we will know how much of us God has by our giving: "For where your treasure is, there your heart will be also" (Matthew 6:21 NIV). Giving is a form of true worship that Satan loves to pervert. There is a right way to worship and a wrong way to worship, and the Tempter knows that. Though God is not a respecter of persons, He is a respecter of offerings. There are offerings that He does not look upon with favor. There are offerings that make Him feel robbed. He has no regard for these offerings because they are not given with a right heart: "true worshipers will worship the Father in spirit and truth" (John 4:23 NIV).

When Ananias and Sapphira sold their property, as told in the book of Acts, they lied to Peter and said they were giving the full amount they had received. Peter responded, "Ananias, why has Satan filled your heart? You lied to the Holy Spirit, and you kept some of the money for yourself. The property was yours to sell or not to sell, as you wished. And after selling it, the money was yours to give away" (Acts 5:3-4 NLT).

Think about it. How would you feel if someone brought you a present that consisted of a set of four plates, but the giver kept one dish and told you the set was complete? However, you had admired the same set at the store, and you knew there was a piece missing! Kinda takes the joy out of it, doesn't it? It completely spoils the spirit of the gift. No wonder "God loves a cheerful giver" (2 Corinthians 9:7 NIV). No one wants a gift given to them "grudgingly, or of necessity" (2 Corinthians 9:7 KJV).

Yet for the sake of appearances, Ananias and Sapphira felt the need to lie. After all, everyone else had been selling their homes and property; they were all living co-op and having a wonderful time. Acts 4:32 says, "All the believers were of one heart and mind, and they felt that what they owned was not their own; they shared everything they had. And the apostles gave powerful witness to the resurrection of the Lord Jesus, and God's great favor was upon them all. There was no poverty among them, because people who owned land or houses sold them and brought the money to the apostles to give to others in need" (NLT). Wow! What a concept! There was no poverty because everyone shared and shared alike.

Obviously, this was a bit overwhelming to Ananias and Sapphira. They liked the idea; they just couldn't bring themselves to buy into it completely. Perhaps they reasoned that they should just keep a little on the side in case this communal living arrangement didn't work out. But they forgot who they were dealing with. Peter was quick to remind them that they were not lying to him, but to God. The consequence for this was death. Needless death, since no one had asked them for their money in the first place. Was it the love of money or the love of what it could buy that was the root of evil in this case?

Jesus made the sobering observation that "it is easier for a camel to go through the eye of a needle than for a rich man to enter the kingdom of God" (Matthew 19:24 NIV). Why? Because their "god is their appetite...and all they think about is this life here on earth" (Philippians 3:19 NLT). A cruel thing for Jesus to say? Not really, when you understand where He was coming from.

Historical rumor has it that within the city wall was a small pedestrian gate. When a merchant got to the city after a certain hour, he found the main gates closed. In order to get his cargo into the city, he had to use the pedestrian gate, which meant he had to completely unpack his camel. The camel then lowered itself and crawled through the small gate. It was impossible for the camel to get through while still carrying all of its cargo; the space was too small. Therefore, the idea behind Jesus' words is that we must be willing to unload everything that keeps us from entering into the presence of God. Many who are used to plenty find this a difficult proposition.

Where Your Heart Is...

The young rich man was all set to follow Jesus until Jesus mentioned selling everything he had. The Bible says he "went away grieved: for he had great possessions" (Mark 10:22 KJV). Many of us are guilty of the same thing. We want to give up, give away, or give God that which we want to give, that which we think we can afford, that which costs us nothing monetarily or otherwise. It only suits us to give what we are willing to part with, but when God oversteps His divine boundaries and asks us to give what we hold precious...well, that becomes a dilemma! Surely He cannot be serious. We know that, being the kind, loving God He is, He'll be happy with whatever we give Him. Hmm...seems a few people found out that was not the case at all. Cain was admonished and punished. Abihu and Nadab were consumed. The priests in the book of Malachi were sharply reprimanded, their offering rejected. Worse yet, they were cursed. This leads me to conclude that God is pretty fussy about His offerings. And well He should be! He Himself gave the ultimate offering—His only begotten Son. Yet many feel they are doing God a favor by throwing Him crumbs and leftovers of what they possess, as well as themselves, while others just think they have a better idea about how to use those offerings.

But if God is the God who owns the cattle on a thousand hills, why is He so concerned about a stupid little offering? What could a lousy little ten percent do for him? Even Uncle Sam asks for more—and gives much less in return, mind you. Ten percent! That's a mere drop in the bucket in the scheme of heavenly wealth. But giving is worship, as well as a testimony of our faith. It takes faith to please God. It was *by faith* that Abel offered God a more acceptable sacrifice (see Hebrews 11:4), and it goes much deeper than that. This same verse goes on to say that Abel was commended as a righteous man because God approved of his offering. And through that offering, though Abel was dead, he continued to speak. His blood cried out to God because he was precious to the Lord.

Why was Abel precious? Because he was a man of faith, he was pleasing to God: "Precious in the sight of the LORD is the death of his saints" (Psalms 116:15 NIV). Another translation says, "His loved ones are very precious to him and he does not lightly let them die."[7] God delights in those who have faith in Him. Right offerings are proof of faith. And we know faith is the last thing the devil wants us to have. Why? Because faith causes us to be obedient, and that defeats his whole purpose.

Only in reference to giving does God invite us to test Him. Don't you find that interesting? He knows some of us can really get hung up on this offering thing, so He gives us an extra clause to work with, saying, in essence, "You don't believe Me? Try Me, and see if I can't return what you give to Me with interest!" (see Malachi 3:10). But then the Tempter whispers in your ear, "Oh, what's the use? How much more money do you have for tithing? You know that ten percent adds up. You could pay a bill with that money. Think about it! The light company is not going to listen when you tell them, 'I put the money I owed you in church, but I'm trusting God....'" He wants you to conclude, "It is vain to serve God: and what profit is it that we have kept his ordinance...?" (Malachi 3:14 KJV).

The Door of Legal Entry

Well, just in case you don't know, I'll tell you what Temptation doesn't want you to know. He doesn't want you to know that the Lord pays heed to those who fear Him, nor does he want you to know that He keeps a book of remembrance filled with all the details on you and what you do. According to Psalm 20, in the day of trouble He will defend you, strengthen you, and send help because He will *remember your offerings,* accept them, and fulfill the desires of your heart. That is what all of this is about. The bottom line is this: Satan is still out to rob you of your blessings and prevent the favor and purposes of God from being manifest in your life. After all, God promises to "rebuke the devourer for your sakes" (Malachi 3:11 KJV) if you are obedient and pay your tithe. It is Temptation's job to make you the robber so that he can then have the legal right to rob you blind.

Since Temptation and the Accuser are tight buddies, as soon as Temptation finishes convincing some poor victim that he needs to hold on to the offering that had been set aside for God so it can be put to better use, Temptation whips out his cell phone and calls the Accuser. "Get Robbery down here quick," Temptation says. "I got him, but I don't know how long I can hold him." And before the poor guy knows it, the money Temptation convinced him to use to pay a bill disappears anyway. Meanwhile, the Accuser stands before God, pointing gleefully at his victim and proclaiming, "I've caught him in the act of disobedience! He has opened the door and invited me in to rob him." And God, who can't go against His Word, has no grounds to tell Robbery, "Hands off."

No wonder the devil was so disgruntled with Job. Job gave offerings *just in case* he, or anyone else in his family, did anything wrong. And truly God rebuked the devourer for his sake. The man was busting out on the right and the left with wealth. Even Satan acknowledged that God had cut him off at the pass, and that he was not allowed access to steal from Job or harm him in any way. I've heard a lot of pastors preach that it was Job's fear that caused calamity to break loose in his life, but I beg to differ. If that had been the case, Satan would have been quick to bring that up and use it as grounds for legal entry to attack Job.

What exactly did Job fear? He never stopped having faith in God. His own wife suggested he curse God and die, but he wouldn't: "I know that my redeemer liveth, and that he shall stand at the latter day upon the earth" (Job 19:25 KJV). That doesn't sound like a lack of faith to me. Job never stopped believing that God was who He said He was. I believe he felt it was God's prerogative to give and to take away. And who was Job to think he deserved to keep what he had? I think he understood that there are seasons in the lives of everyone when we are tested and tried; these seasons are part of the cycle of life. It is how we deal with the test that determines the end result of our circumstance.

Let's keep in mind that this whole situation with Job started because God was so delighted with Job's righteousness. According to the book of Hebrews, back in those days, faith was accounted to the believers as righteousness. In Galatians 3:6, we see that this was the basis of Abraham's righteousness: "Abraham believed in God, so God declared him righteous because of his faith" (NLT). Satan wants none of that going on. Oh, what a tangled web we weave when first we practice to deceive! Who would have ever thought that a simple little offering could hold so many other issues in the balance?

Where Your Treasure Is

No Christian is safe. Judas, who walked and talked with Jesus daily, became a victim of Temptation. In this particular situation, offerings were once again involved. Jesus, along with His disciples, went to visit Lazarus, a man He raised from the dead (see John 12:1-8). In this account we find Lazarus' two sisters, Mary and Martha, engaged in very opposite pursuits. Martha is busy serving, while Mary is adoring Jesus. Martha takes pride in serving; Mary understands the value of worship. Even today, many in the body of Christ confuse worship and serving. This is another favorite playground of the enemy's. He wants us to get so caught up in the *doing* that we forget all about *being*. We must *be* who God has called us to be—worshipers.

In the first account of Martha and Mary, which you can read about in Luke 10:38-42, Martha is a little bit miffed. While she's doing all the work, Mary has contented herself by simply enjoying Jesus' company. When Martha asks Jesus to chastise Mary for not helping, He replies to Martha that she troubles herself with too much activity—activity that is not conducive to her experiencing blessings or joy. Mary, on the other hand, chose the better part that will not be taken away from her. Her experience with Jesus would be lasting.

So many have mourned in anguish the passing of those near and dear because they never spent quality time or shared their heart with the departed person. So many words unsaid, so many questions left unanswered. In sharp contrast, others stand at the graveside with serene looks upon their faces, recalling memories of countless hours spent with this dear person—special moments filled with laughter, shared confidences, and tears. They will cherish these things that will never pass away and treasure them forever.

Mary really loved Jesus. She was a true worshiper who treasured the times she spent with her Savior. She was willing

to give her all—her attention, her affections, and her offerings. And so, on another very special evening, she chose to
pour a pint of pure nard—a very expensive ointment—on the
feet of Jesus. Humbling herself even further, she wiped His
feet with her hair. Well, Judas thought this was the most
ridiculous thing he had ever seen. He objected, saying, "Why
wasn't this perfume sold and the money given to the poor? It
was worth a year's wages" (John 12:5 NIV). But the Bible then
goes on to explain in verse 6, "He did not say this because he
cared about the poor but because he was a thief; as keeper
of the money bag, he used to help himself to what was put
into it" (NIV).

Aha! Just the entryway Temptation needed to pull off his
ultimate plot—getting rid of Jesus. (Or so he thought.) The
very next chapter reveals that while Jesus washed the disciples'
feet before the Last Supper, the devil had already put it into
the heart of Judas to betray Jesus (see John 13:2). Later,
during the dinner, after Judas had communion with Jesus,
Satan entered into him (see verse 27). And the rest is history.
Judas then left to betray Jesus.

Poor Judas! He was played like a fiddle. First Temptation
blinded him. He never saw Jesus for who He really was.
Judas came to the party with his own agenda. From where
Judas stood, if Jesus really were the Savior, He was supposed
to save the Jews from Roman oppression. To Judas, all of this
heaven-bound talk was for the birds. This twisted insight did
nothing for his attitude toward worship. Sound familiar? Satan
did the same thing. He, too, decided he was entitled to take
a little of that worship for himself. *Forget God's agenda,* he
thought. *I will pacify myself with what I can get in my own
power since He refuses to line up with my agenda.* And so,
this train of thought and behavior continued until the rebellious heart found itself completely shipwrecked. We too will
be disappointed if we decide to follow Christ in an effort to

fulfill our own agenda. That disappointment will lead us to crucify Him afresh with our own willfulness, only to find ourselves more dissatisfied.

Judas betrayed Jesus and was overcome with so much condemnation that he couldn't bear to keep the money he'd earned for his filthy little task. He wanted to return the money to its rightful place, but it had become sour to all involved in this little escapade. It was too late. It was an unacceptable offering. Even the priests who wanted Jesus out of the way knew that. In the dawning realization of the depth of his actions, Condemnation screamed louder at him than the voice of Conviction calling him to repent, and Judas committed suicide—spiritually, as well as physically. And the walls of hell rang with laughter at this senseless fool who left himself so open for Temptation.

In Hindsight

So many find themselves in this predicament. God doesn't move fast enough to grant them the desires of their heart, so they let it affect their worship. They begin to cut back on what they give to God, reasoning that they need to fill in the gaps for themselves. This is just the opportunity Temptation waits for to invite Sin into the picture. Soon the hapless victims find themselves too far out at sea, drifting on the reckless waves of Self-indulgence. Somewhere along the way, they lose their oars and find themselves no longer steering the boat, swept away by forces greater than their own. More often than not, when they crash, they blame God as the culprit who caused all their misfortune and the awful consequences they suffered.

But who is the real culprit? Is it really Temptation, or is it your own heart? I would venture to say that the culprit is definitely the heart, better known as your will. "Out of the heart come evil thoughts, murder, adultery, sexual immorality, theft, false testimony, slander. These are what make a man 'unclean'" (Matthew 15:19 NIV). Temptation is merely a suave suitor who tantalizes the seat of your passion with delectable promises of what it already desires. "But God promises to give me the desires of my heart!" you cry. Yes, this is true. But take a look at the beginning of that particular verse. In fact, back up one more verse: "Trust in the LORD, and do good; so shalt thou dwell in the land, and verily thou shalt be fed. Delight thyself also in the LORD; and he shall give thee the desires of thine heart" (Psalm 37:3-4 KJV). *Trust. Do good. Delight in the Lord.* These are the steps that lead to worship, the steps that lead to blessing!

Could this be why the very first question Satan proposed in the garden was, "Hath God said...?" (Genesis 3:1 NKJV). He pulls out his trusty little shovel and starts digging away at the base of our trust in God. Temptation arrives with flowers to pay the heart a visit, inviting it to come and play. And who wants to worship when they are playing in the fields of self-will? But then darkness falls, and we are forced to come inside and petulantly question why our desires haven't been granted.

Even the Bible attests that "hope deferred makes the heart sick" (Proverbs 13:12 NKJV). It's hard to be delighted with God when He hasn't done what we feel He should. What could He possibly be waiting for? How about this: "After you have done the will of God, you may receive the promise" (Hebrews 10:36 NKJV). But what is the will of God? Pure worship and unadulterated obedience: "If you love Me, keep My commandments" (John 14:15 NKJV). There's that heart thing again. I think it's safe to conclude the misguided desires of the heart are the true culprit in mankind's downward spiral. Temptation is a mere accessory to the crime, and he's given way more credit than he is due.

Many have interpreted "God will give you the desires of your heart" as saying that God will actually plant the desire there, and because He agrees with the desire, He will then grant you the fulfillment of it. I disagree on the grounds that He made us free agents. If it were true that He manipulates our hearts, He would cause everyone to desire salvation. What I've found to be true is that when we get to the place of real worship—the type of worship that is genuine in spirit and in truth—something happens. Our desires change; they become more God-centered, they fit in with God's design for our lives. Our desires become the types of desires that He can honor because they line up with His Word, His divine purposes for our lives, and the work of the kingdom.

Would God allow us to have access to something we should not have? Yes indeed! (He did it with Adam and Eve.) Why? To teach us to master our fleshly impulses and test our hearts. And to reveal to us what we are really worshiping.

I'm reminded of the worship chorus that says, "When I look into your holiness, when I gaze into your loveliness, when all things that surround become shadows in the light of you..."[8] All of the selfish gesticulations of the heart come to a screeching halt when we enter into true worship. The heart is no longer susceptible to Temptation because it is lost in the glory of an all-consuming God, "caught up in the rapture of love." And when we are truly in love, we want only what our lover wants.

Worship is the secret place that hides the heart from the advances of the enemy. Worship will make even the most vulnerable heart spurn the flirtations of Temptation. Worship causes the heart to slip through the snare of the snake. Why? Because Satan's rap is old. We've seen his moves before. "That which has been is what will be, that which is done is what will be done, and there is nothing new under the sun" (Ecclesiastes 1:9 NKJV). The devil is still up to the same old tricks. Those who dip into the offering plate and skim off the worship are still unwittingly victimized by the deception of their own hearts.

9

RISING FROM THE DUST

"For if our heart condemn us, God is greater than
our heart..."

1 JOHN 3:20 KJV

THE HEART IS A RESILIENT MUSCLE," a famous director once
said. Sometimes the aftereffects of sin can be more devastating than the consequences of the fall itself. Temptation
counts on that. He is quick to tell you, "You've torn your
britches beyond repair, and God will never forgive you for
what you've done." This is where many people lose steam
and peter out in the race, landing in a pit of depression. The
Tempter knows if he can get you to indulge yourself in disobedience and then throw it back in your face, he can snuff
out your relationship with God, thereby cutting you off at the
path to recovery. Remember how Adam and Eve ran and hid
after their little snack in the garden? Remember Cain's deeper
plummet into sin when God tried to correct him? I wonder
why it always feels easier to resign than to repent.

We are a generation who will avoid confession at any cost. In the long run, however, the cost is unavoidable. People appear on talk shows every day, attributing their bad habits to the things they endured as children at the hands of their parents, or blaming the gene pool. Such deceptions, temporarily, at least, seem comforting. "The apple doesn't fall far from the tree," we resolve. "Like father, like son," we sigh. Oh, we've come up with all sorts of little sayings to explain away our tendencies that seem to run in the family. But to be perfectly honest, if we survey what the Word of God says, we'll discover this is a weak cop-out.

Generational Curses: Fact or Fiction?

Let's see...the favorite Scriptures for this argument are found in Exodus 20: "I the LORD thy God am a jealous God, *visiting the iniquity* of the fathers upon the children unto the third and fourth generation *of them that hate me;* and *showing mercy* unto thousands of *them that love me*, and *keep my commandments*" (verses 5-6 KJV, emphasis added). What exactly does this mean? What exactly is a curse? Well, Webster's describes a curse as "a prayer or invocation for harm or injury to come upon one," "evil or misfortune that comes as if in response to imprecation or as retribution," or "a cause of great harm or misfortune." So, in layman's English, we can break this down to understand that a curse is brought on an individual by the spoken order of another or as payment for a deed deserving of a curse. *For a deed deserving of a curse* becomes the operative phrase here. The door must be opened in order for a curse to enter into the house of your life and set up residence. Remember when Balaam was sent to curse the Israelites? This verse rings with a potent promise to all believers: "How can I curse those whom God has not cursed? How can I condemn those whom the LORD has not condemned?" (Numbers 23:8 NLT). You are now the blessed of God; you are, therefore, the gatekeeper to your own life. Disobedience to the Word of God is what Temptation counts on to give "cause" to curses in your life. *Disobedience* is the one who opens the door and invites in harmless-looking guests who come bearing housewarming gifts of bondage. We must also conclude that curses are a reality. Because all of mankind became cursed under the law, there was no way for man to uphold all of God's commands. This is why we needed Christ to redeem us from the curse of the law by becoming a curse for us: "For it is written: 'Cursed is everyone who is hung on a tree'" (Galatians 3:13 NIV). But what about this issue of God *"visiting* the iniquity of the fathers upon the children"? Let's just consider the word *"visiting."* Does everyone who comes to visit your home stay? No! Not unless you invite them to. Remember, "A curse without cause shall not alight" (Proverbs 26:2 NKJV). In order to perpetrate his agenda, Satan counts on you having the same tendencies and desires as your parents and forefathers. In most cases, generational *habits* are misconstrued as generation curses. Sons and daughters adopt the same unhealthy habits as their parents and reap the same undesirable results. But now you can transform your life by the renewing of your mind. Through the blood of Jesus you are now free to break that cycle in your life.

I know a young lady whose aunt predicted that she would be "just like her mother" and bear a child out of wedlock. Where this statement came from she never understood, because this was not a pattern in her family. Perhaps the aunt came to this conclusion based on the young lady's experimental behavior at the time. But it's comments like these that have caused many to stumble. The Bible says that "death and life are in the power of the tongue: and they that love it shall eat the fruit thereof" (Proverbs 18:21 KJV). We can curse people with our mouths while the enemy lies in wait for the opportunity to put the curse into effect, but he must have scriptural grounds in order to do so.

In Genesis 49:4, Jacob, using his spiritual authority as a parent, pronounced that Reuben would never excel, and the tribe of Reuben lived up to that decree. Let's take a look at what Jacob said. He made a pronouncement based on what he had observed of Reuben throughout a lifetime. He knew his son. And he knew that Reuben had slept with one of his wives. He said, "Unstable as water, you shall not excel, because you went up to your father's bed; then you defiled it" (NKJV). Not only was Jacob basing his words on the major character flaw he saw firmly cemented in the foundation of Reuben's character, he was instinctively lining up with an even greater scriptural principle that hadn't been written yet: "Honor your father and your mother, as the LORD your God has commanded you, so that you may live long and that it may go well with you" (Deuteronomy 5:16 NIV).

Reuben dishonored his father and had settled into being a man without character. Remember, words have power, especially the words of a parent. Yet the bottom line remains—the curse had "cause" to alight. And generations later, the tribe of Reuben continued to adopt the standard (or iniquity) that Reuben had established in his own life. Faced with the same circumstance in her own life, the aforementioned young lady could have fulfilled her aunt's prophecy, but she slammed the door when the curse came knocking. She chose to honor God and honor her parents, to inherit blessings instead of curses. Today she stands as a testimony to the power of the blood of Jesus Christ.

Now at the age of forty, though still single, she has no children because she submitted herself to God's call to remain celibate until marriage. Yes, Temptation has "visited" her with situations that could have made her aunt's prophecy a reality. But, by the grace of God, she resisted and remained obedient to God's Word.

We have seen generations of families locked into cycles of poverty, drug addiction, illegitimate births, crime, and other problems. And then one stellar member of the family breaks away from the pack and becomes an upstanding, successful member of society. How do we explain this? What is the difference between this one person and the rest of the family? *The power of choice.* The iniquities of our fathers can only remain and affect our lives if we invite them in when they come to the door.

Breaking Family Tradition

In Scripture it's clear to see that lust ran in David's family and lying ran in Abraham's family. Remember? Abraham lied that Sarah was his sister, then his son, Isaac, told the same lie about his wife Rebekah when faced with the same circumstances. Isaac then had Jacob, and Jacob lied and stole the blessing. Then Jacob had sons, and they lied to the people of Schechem. They also lied about what happened to their brother Joseph. (Well, those brothers told several big, fat lies.) But wait a minute! There's no record of Joseph lying. Did this propensity for lying skip over a brother? No, I'm sure it didn't. I would surmise that Joseph had several occasions pop up in his life where a lie would have helped him get what he wanted, but he made a different *choice.*

We must keep in mind that God is a fair God. He punishes people for their own sins, per Deuteronomy 24:16: "The fathers shall not be put to death for the children, neither shall the children be put to death for the fathers: every man shall be put to death for his own sin" (KJV). That's pretty basic, but just in case you're not convinced, take a look at Ezekiel 18:2-32. Let's start at the beginning and take our time with this passage. God starts off by saying, "Behold, all souls are mine; as the soul of the father, so also the soul of the son is mine: the soul that sinneth, it shall die" (verse 4 KJV). Another translation states that "the life of the father is like the life of the son, both are mine, only the one who sins shall die."[9] He then goes on to say that if a righteous father has a son who is unrighteous (I'm paraphrasing), the unrighteous son shall die and his blood will be upon him (see verse 13). In other words, the son is responsible for his own death, or, "his death shall be his own fault."[10]

The passage goes on to say, "But suppose this son has a son who sees all the sins his father commits, and though he sees them, he does not do such things....He will not die for his father's sin; he will surely live" (verses 14,17 NIV, emphasis added). Obviously this whole generational curse thing was an issue even back in Old Testament days because God took His time to painstakingly clarify His point. He did not want people using Exodus 20:5 in the wrong context as a scapegoat for their actions. God continues His rationale in Ezekiel 18:2-3,19-20: "What do you people mean by quoting this proverb about the land of Israel: 'The fathers eat sour grapes, and the children's teeth are set on edge'? As surely as I live, declares the Sovereign LORD, you will no longer quote this proverb in Israel....Yet you ask, 'Why does the son not share the guilt of his father?' Since the son has done what is just and right and has been careful to keep all my decrees, he will surely live. The soul who sins is the one who will die. The son will not share the guilt of the father" (NIV). In essence, according to another translation, "Only the one who sins shall die."[11] The end, by God.

So what's the final nitty-gritty on this subject? We do not inherit curses; God is not into punishing the innocent. *However*, if you, of your own volition, choose to follow in the footsteps of your parents, imitating their established patterns of behavior that is not conducive to victorious living according to God's standards, then you will reap the same consequences as your parents. No spiritual technicality binds and obligates children to repeat the mistakes of their fathers or mothers. If this chain-reaction theory were correct, then it would stand to reason that all righteous parents would have perfectly righteous children, and we know this is not the case. In the end, we all make our own beds to lie in.

We must take stock of the things we do consciously and subconciously that bear results that we do not like in our lives. Are they things our parents did? Have destructive modes of behavior become "normal" simply because that was the way you always saw it being done? It's time to break the chains and begin a new tradition. Just because Papa was a rolling stone doesn't mean you have to be one. Just because mama was a hard, cold woman who chased men away with her caustic tongue doesn't mean you have to continue the cycle of broken relationships and bitterness. Get the picture?

Though it may be hard to fathom that good ol' mom and dad did some things that weren't considered spiritually correct in the eyes of God, we cannot choose to rationalize that if they did it, then it must be all right. God says no deal. We must be responsible for our own standard of living before Him. We can slide along the ruler from trying to do the right thing and missing the mark, to saying, "I can't stand it any longer; I'm just gonna do my own thing," to finally settling in the place of a seared conscience loudly proclaiming, "Hey, what's all the fuss about? There's nothing wrong with what I'm doing. You people need to lighten up and realize that times are changing." But it makes no difference to God; sin is still sin. As with the act of murder, whether accidental or premeditated, murder still means there is a victim who is dead, and somebody is going to pay. There's no hiding behind mom and dad when it comes to receiving your own share of the consequences.

Now, it *is* possible for children to suffer directly from the sins of their parents. Crack babies, for instance, often suffer physically and mentally because of the unhealthy habits of their parents. Hereditary diseases are another issue that we cannot ignore. Some diseases or conditions can be avoided if we pay proper attention to our lifestyle and diet. Diabetes runs in my family, so I watch my intake of sweets and take care of myself. I'm happy to say that I don't have even a hint of diabetes.

A famous singer, Patti Labelle, was interviewed a while back. She was sharing her feelings concerning the premature death of all the women in her family due to breast cancer. At the time of the interview she was really struggling with fear because she was approaching the age when the rest of the women in her family had died. Today she is well past this dreaded age, and she gives the glory for her healthy life to God for His healing power and His ability to keep her safe. Some children are not so fortunate and do suffer the maladies of their parents. However, these are the natural consequences of sin being in the world. It's like living in a smoggy city—you're going to breathe in some of the pollution whether you want to or not.

To some extent we cannot escape being unwitting victims of circumstance. I believe this is why Jesus said, "In the world you will have tribulation; but be of good cheer, I have overcome the world" (John 16:33 NKJV). Problems and sickness will come, but these things should not be put under the umbrella of generational curses. We should be careful not to become like Job's friends, diagnosing the illness wrongly.

Sometimes people's illnesses can be attributed to no particular cause or person, as we see in John 9:1-3: "As he [Jesus] went along, he saw a man blind from birth. His disciples asked him, 'Rabbi, who sinned, this man or his parents, that he was born blind?' 'Neither this man nor his parents sinned,' said Jesus, 'but this happened so that the work of God might be displayed in his life'" (NIV). Jesus then went on to cure the blind man. God is always seeking an opportunity to glorify Himself in a changed life, to lift someone above the odds. No one has to settle into unvictorious patterns of living just because the domino theory running rampant through a family has caused all to conclude, "Well, that's just the way things are in this family. There's no way out." I dare say there *is* a way out. Through the blood of Jesus, the path has been cleared to secure liberty and break generational chains.

Please do not think that I am dismissing the reality of spiritual warfare. Absolutely not. That would be unscriptural. The Bible gives many instances of mental and physical conditions that were caused by spirits that needed to be cast out. And the casting out freed the victims. Many people do suffer from the oppression of demonic entities. For me to delve into that arena would require another book, so I shall stay focused on the subject of temptation. My position is this: We as believers do not have to entertain the devil and give him access to our lives. The blood of Jesus has given us a choice. It is our choice to resist the devil and submit ourselves to God so that Satan will flee from our lives and circumstances. It is not by the design of some cosmic decision without any say-so from you. We have been given authority to "overcome the power of the enemy" (Luke 10:19 NIV). We are now able to overcome Satan through "the blood of the Lamb and by the word of [our] testimony" (Revelation 12:11 NIV). There is no need for us to entertain Satan and give him permission to wreak havoc in our lives.

Because we belong to Jesus, we have the power to allow or disallow satanic influence or suggestions to take root in our lives. You *do not* have to be like your mother; you *do not* have to be like your father; you don't have to be like anybody but Jesus! Wow! Isn't that liberating? The truth is the light, so walk in it.

Under the Magnifying Glass

Now that we've decided not to blame anyone else for our state of affairs, let's get realistic about where we really live. After all is said and done, our state of slipping into or out of darkness is entirely up to us. We are instructed to "submit yourselves, then, to God, resist the devil, and he will flee from you" (James 4:7 NIV). But just in case you don't, and you find yourself staring at Condemnation, who delights in magnifying all your sins before you, don't fall for Temptation's next set of tricks. He's designed these to make you sink lower and lower into self instead of reaching up to God for help. And this is exactly where Temptation wants you. He wants you to feel that you have no right to call on God for anything now that you've proven to Him what a filthy, good-for-nothing sinner you are. Or, even worse, Temptation gets you believing that you're the only person in the world who specializes in your own unique brand of sin. You, unlike everyone else, are absolutely hopeless.

There isn't a more helpless feeling than when you've been wrongly accused of something. People say that time reveals all things, but at the moment of accusation, that's not good enough. You want proof that will clear your reputation, and you want it *now!*

In the face of accusation, our first reaction is to defend ourselves with any sort of justification we can come up with. Self-justification in the face of condemnation is like quicksand. The more you wiggle, the deeper you sink. Along these lines, I had a devastating experience shortly before I came to Christ. I was dating a man, and we had a huge argument one evening. He decided to take a vacation in order to cool off. While he was on this vacation, he was shot and died shortly after from the wound. When his best friend called to inform me that he was in the hospital and probably would not make it, his parting words to me were, "It's all your fault. If it wasn't for you, this wouldn't have happened." These words stuck in my craw and worked me overtime. I struggled with the burden of guilt for years. Every time I experienced another failed relationship with a man, I would chalk it up to the fact that I didn't deserve a good relationship because I'd botched my relationship with my former boyfriend so badly.

I didn't feel I had the right to ask God to bring someone significant into my life; I was undeserving. Get the picture? Yielding to Temptation paralyzes us and hinders us from receiving the blessings of God. It shuts down our prayer life and renders us helpless and ineffective. Even though God is the first One we should run to, our guilt works against us like the big bully at school who threatens, "I'm gonna get you if you tell!"

I recall another frustrating incident when I said something about someone that I shouldn't have said. (It was a true statement, but I shouldn't have said it.) Someone else then took what I said, twisted it, and told the person I said something completely different—far more terrible than what I had really said. I was mortified! I found it hard to pray for vindication because I felt I deserved to be punished for saying anything at all. How could I now ask God to help me? I had not taken the whole pie, but I had certainly stuck my finger in it. And now I looked guilty because of one little blueberry stain. There was no explaining it away. So I decided to admit to what I had said—as embarrassing as even that was—and leave it up to God to sort out the rest of the lies that had been told.

The Key to Freedom

And therein lies the secret—*confession*. The day I sat in a Bill Gothard Basic Youth Conflicts seminar and learned that secret was the beginning of the rest of my life, as far as I was concerned. This was where all my inner turmoil and all the arguments and justifications over the death of my boyfriend ended. No more attempting to reason, "He decided to take a trip out of anger toward me; I didn't make him go. He's a grown man. I didn't pull the trigger." None of that mattered after I learned that guilt is a function of the spirit, not of the intellect. There is no way to run away from your own spirit. Just think of all those people who spend hundreds of dollars an hour to lie on a therapist's couch, trying to find justification for their soiled consciences, when all they have to do is own up to it and move on! Well, there's one more important component here—the blood of Jesus. When I put all the parts together, I was finally released to say, "You're right, Satan. I did contribute to his death with my actions. I am guilty. My caustic behavior drove him to a place that put him in danger and I will never do that to anyone again. But that is why Jesus died on the cross for me, and I accept His death as payment for my guilt."

I cannot explain the feeling of release that came over me as I made this confession. It almost seemed too simple. But there it was—forgiveness flooding down over me, washing me clean, soothing my conscience, chasing away my fears and my feelings of being soiled and unworthy to receive anything from God. Ah, yes, confession is good for the soul. This is why Temptation hates to see us confess. Guilt keeps us in anticipation of punishment. Our days become filled with fear as we wait for the other shoe to drop. It's like a prankster pulling his last trick on a friend, who then threatens to reciprocate, uttering those famous last words: "I'm going to get you for that!" The prankster now feels he's got to stay on his toes. After all, he doesn't know when the retaliation will occur. Waiting for the payback can actually be much more horrifying than experiencing the actual act of retribution.

Does anybody ever really get away with anything? We think escaping punishment means that we're not caught openly, but I beg to differ with the masses. What about the torture of hiding what you've done because the information is far too explosive to share with anyone? It's almost impossible to keep something so terrible hidden. This is why people get caught for crimes they seemingly could have gotten away with. They left no clues at the scene of the crime, but the weight of their guilt was too much for them to bear in silence, so they told one person and that person squealed. I've always wondered in those cases, how could they have been so stupid? Yet, it isn't stupidity or even a sense of bravado that pressures them to tell someone. It is the sheer weight of condemnation that crushes the admission out of them.

I recall one incident when I was away from home and had some friends staying at my place. One of them accidentally tipped over an urn that was on a pedestal and broke part of it. Another friend recommended moving the unbroken portion to the front and placing some items in the urn to hide the break. But my poor guilty friend couldn't take it. The moment I called from out of town, he blurted out, "I broke your urn in the hallway! I'm so sorry!" My other friend, feigning disdain, said he would never do anything wrong in the presence of my poor guilt-ridden buddy because he wasn't a good sinner; he folded too easily. We had quite a laugh about it, but the principle was deep. Thank the Lord for my friend's tender conscience. He is a wonderful Christian who walks carefully before God.

Can you imagine committing a crime and then watching on television as the clues begin to pile up, bringing the detectives closer and closer to you? Imagine the sleepless nights, the jumping at the slightest sound, the looking over your shoulder constantly. And just when you think you'd gotten away with it and exhaled in relief—BAM! You're hit with the spotlight of discovery.

As I was traveling with the group I mentioned earlier, an interesting thing occurred. At one of the hotels, someone in our group was accused of stealing a light fixture from his room. Well, we just couldn't believe this guy would do such a thing, so we all rallied to the defense of our wrongly accused friend. As the trip continued, I noticed him becoming very defensive over the slightest comments and taking personal affront to the most innocent of jokes. He felt that everyone was snidely accusing him of thievery. I couldn't understand why he was reading this into comments that, from my perspective, in no way alluded to stealing. Later I found out he actually *had* taken the thing he was accused of stealing. Then it all made sense to me. Poor thing! His nerves must have been completely raw by the end of the trip. Although it had been a long trip for us all, I'm sure he was the one who was most relieved when it was over.

But sin affects everyone in the vicinity. Imagine the anger, disgust, and disappointment those who had defended him felt when they discovered the truth of the matter. It was difficult to keep from taking it upon ourselves to confront, judge, and humble him. Although we reached the conclusion that it was God's job to deal with his conscience, it put a strain—and, in many cases, a permanent rift—on friendships that had grown throughout our time together. What a waste, in light of how the trip started out.

Escaping the Grip of Condemnation

"There is therefore now no condemnation to those who are in Christ Jesus, who do not walk according to the flesh, but according to the Spirit" (Romans 8:1 NKJV). Though I have been very tongue-in-cheek when illustrating Satan's conversations concerning you, let me get very serious with you for a moment. Never underestimate the genius of your foe. Never relax and view this hateful adversary as harmless. Satan is serious about his mission to destroy you. It only takes one look at the daily papers to see that.

No life is sacred to Satan. He doesn't care who you are. As a matter of fact, he likes high-level visibility. The better to bring you down, my dear. Be assured, if he has any inkling of your future, he will set you up and wait for your golden moment of destiny. And then, as you are about to plunge that flag into the summit of your purpose, he will rise up with a "Remember when..." to wipe the smile of victory off your face and silence the accolades of those around you. Temptation is patient; he will draw out his game like a long-play music mix. You never know how much energy you exerted dancing to it until the record ends and you fall down in a heap of exhaustion. Yes, even having a good time can take its toll on you. Temptation knows this, and he plans his strategy well. Do yourself a favor—don't underestimate him. Even the angels in heaven know better.

A minister friend of mine once told me that she guarded and protected her marriage with a vengeance. Why? Because she and her husband's major ministry emphasis is marriage and family. She knows that Satan would love to ruin her marriage and her family, making them a laughingstock to all they ministered to. What better way to annihilate the effects of their ministry and get them to sit down and shut up? Satan would much rather see them scrambling to repair their own house instead of helping build homes for others. My friend said, "Every morning when I wake up, I ask the Lord, 'Okay, where is he and what is he planning?' I intend to stay a step ahead of the devil." Now, that's good! We as Christians need to become offensive with the devil instead of running around in a last-minute panic, always on the defensive, a day late and a dollar short.

From Behind the Eight Ball

But because most of us are not ahead of the game, let's deal with how to repair the breaches before we move on to getting a step ahead of our foe. Paul—who we first came to know as Saul—had the nerve to say this in one of his dissertations: "Men and brethren, I have lived in all good conscience before God until this day" (Acts 23:1 KJV). How could he say such a thing? This man had killed Christians! He had been a legalistic, religious zealot! How could he stand there in good conscience and make such a statement? Because Paul had an understanding of what took place at the cross. This was why he was able to write to the Hebrews, "Let us draw near to God with a sincere heart in full assurance of faith, having our hearts sprinkled to cleanse us from a guilty conscience and having our bodies washed with pure water" (Hebrews 10:22 NIV). Paul took the promise of the blood and ran with it. I believe he would have sung with deep conviction one of my favorite hymns: "There is a fountain filled with blood drawn from Emmanuel's veins, and sinners plunged beneath that fount lose all their guilty stains...."

The stain of Christ's blood cancels out the stain of sin—but only in the lives of those who honestly take inventory. The word *repentance* can be broken down as follows: *re* is a prefix meaning "back, again, against, anew, backward," as in *recall, reassess, revisit, return, redo;* and *pent* meaning to *"shut up"* or *"confine." Repentance,* then, is an order to reassess through confession. Revisit your actions and see them through God's eyes, then willfully set boundaries for yourself that keep you from practicing that sin. Confine your will to line up with the Word of God. Remember, confession is only the beginning. What God calls for is a forsaking of the wrong action or attitude. Sin is the outward manifestation of our rebellion. The more we exercise this, the more we are in danger of slipping deeper into the bowels of iniquity, which is a state of heart. You can actually be doing all the right things but harbor iniquity in your heart. Therefore, reassess your heart condition, and make the determination to turn away from all attitudes and practices that are not of God. David, the king of Israel, assessed his own heart and cried out to God, "Create in me a pure heart, O God, and renew a steadfast spirit within me" (Psalm 51:10 NIV). Isaiah assessed his situation and confessed before God that he was a man of unclean lips (see Isaiah 6:5). After confessing this, God sent an angel to touch his lips and cleanse him. God is willing to do the cleansing for us if we are willing to be not just honest with Him, but completely willing to change. "'Come now, let us reason together,' says the LORD. 'Though your sins are like scarlet, they shall be as white as snow; though they are red as crimson, they shall be like wool'" (Isaiah 1:18 NIV).

Paul was quite mindful of the fact that there was no turning back "if we deliberately keep on sinning after we have received the knowledge of the truth, no sacrifice for sins is left, but only a fearful expectation of judgment" (Hebrews 10:26-27 NIV). There's that condemnation thing again, the accusing finger that needles away at your peace, your confidence, and your faith.

When you're on the outs with God, it's hard to believe He has your back. Remember that silly game you played in school when you had to fall back into the arms of your schoolmate—only you never really knew if they would catch you or not? What was the deciding factor? Relationship. Someone who was in your corner would catch you; those who didn't care about you would let you fall. Because we are creatures most prone to conditional love, it's hard for us to grasp the concept that even when we offend God He cares enough to catch us before we go too low. "The steps of the godly are directed by the LORD. He delights in every detail of their lives. Though they stumble, they will not fall, for the LORD holds them by the hand" (Psalm 37:23-24 NLT).

Well, who said I offended God? you may wonder. Every time we sin, we offend God. Sin is an affront to His nature. And it becomes difficult to believe you can now go boldly before the throne and ask for anything else until this little matter between you and God gets cleared up. It's hard to trust someone else when you yourself are not trustworthy. Everything is colored by your projection of your own personal experience. This is why the Word says, "Everything is pure to those whose hearts are pure. But nothing is pure to those who are corrupt and unbelieving, because their minds and consciences are defiled" (Titus 1:15 NLT).

So, how do we crawl out from under the wet blanket of condemnation? How do we regain our confidence and get back in a justified position? "[Repent! And then] let us come boldly to the throne of our gracious God [really meaning business with Him]. There, we will [be sure to] receive His mercy, and we will find grace to help us when we need it…[and then] continue to live in fellowship with Christ so that when He returns, you will be full of courage and not shrink back from Him in shame. [Because you will be sure that you are] justified by faith, [and] have peace with God through [your] Lord Jesus Christ" (Hebrews 4:16; 1 John 2:28; and Romans 5:1—Michelle's paraphrased version).

Then you will be able to freely sing, "He paid a debt He did not owe, I owed a debt I could not pay, I needed someone to wash my sins away. And now I sing a brand-new song, 'Amazing Grace,' Christ Jesus paid the debt that I could never pay…."

There, but for the grace of God, go I. How about you? I once heard a great illustration to explain that grace is being given something we don't deserve and mercy is not being given what we really deserve. The person speaking said, "Grace is when you go, 'Wow!' and Mercy is when you wipe your brow and go, 'Whew!'" I want to get past "Whew!" and graduate to "Way to go!"

So how do you get out from behind the eight ball and get a step ahead of Temptation? The psalmist said it best: *Selah*. Stop and carefully ponder the matter. Before sampling one of those delectable treats that Temptation is sure to wave beneath your nose, consider the cost. No *hors d'oeuvre* is really for free.

10

BETWEEN THE PIT AND THE PALACE

"They are a nation void of counsel, neither is there
any understanding in them. O that they were wise,
that they understood this, that they would consider
their latter end!"

DEUTERONOMY 32:28-29 KJV

WHENEVER I GO TO THE GROCERY STORE, I experience the
same phenomenon. I weave my way through aisle after aisle,
putting things into my grocery cart that may or may not be on
my grocery list. Hmm...a new kind of juice...that looks deli-
cious. Oh, and it's only two dollars! I can handle that. On and
on I go with my eyes growing bigger than my wallet at every
bend. Finally I arrive at the checkout line. And to my horror,
the grand total of my shopping expedition is beyond my
wildest expectations. To be perfectly honest, I never really
considered the total cost as I threw one tantalizing treat after
another into my cart with the utmost of abandon. But the
inevitable tally is always sobering, reminding me once again
that there's a price to pay for everything. Oh, if only we
would apply this theory to our lives! If only we'd learn to

consider the end tally or result. What a novel concept! That is what God calls *wisdom*. But wisdom is not enough. We must arrive at the place of understanding. God says: "The people that doth not understand shall fall" (Hosea 4:14 KJV). Or perhaps you're more familiar with, "My people are destroyed for lack of knowledge" (Hosea 4:6 KJV). Either side of the coin, the take-away is the same. It behooves us to get some wisdom and, with that wisdom, a working understanding of who God is and how His principles apply very practically to our own lives.

I shudder to think that a lot of sin today happens because, for the most part, we've lost our fear of God. One thing I've noticed is that children no longer have the respect for authority they once did. Discipline has taken the form of administering "time-outs" and attempting to reason with those who don't yet have the skills to grasp rationale. A friend of mine recently complained to me that time-outs were just not working with her little daughter. My friend seemed quite befuddled by this. I was not. I asked her to show me where time-outs were in Scripture, and then I showed her the verse that reads, "The rod and reproof give wisdom: but a child left to himself bringeth his mother to shame" (Proverbs 29:15 KJV). She was mortified.

So if our natural parents are wimping out, how can we take our heavenly Parent seriously and have a healthy fear of His chastening? After all, our earthly parents are the only point of reference we have to the concept of God the Father being our Parent.

Many people find it hard to believe that God really means what His Word says in our present shifting times. *Surely He's more flexible than His Word suggests,* we think. Yet the Bible clearly states: "The fear of the LORD is the beginning of wisdom: and the knowledge of the Holy is understanding" (Proverbs 9:10 KJV). Another translation reads, "True wisdom begins with fear of the Lord, he best discerns who has the knowledge of holy things."[12] There was a time when the fear of God alone kept many from living foolishly, but that is an era gone by. And where there is no fear of the Lord, there is no consideration of the consequences of our actions. "It is sport to a fool to do wrong, but wise conduct is pleasure to a man of understanding" (Proverbs 10:23).[13] "Folly is joy to him that is destitute of wisdom: but a man of understanding walketh uprightly" (Proverbs 15:21 KJV). Shall I go on?

I believe there are several components to winning the tug-of-war with Temptation, and we will look at each one carefully. First of all, as I have stated, you must have a healthy reverence and realistic fear of the Lord. King Solomon told his son in Proverbs that this was the beginning of wisdom. God is a loving Father, but He is also a sovereign King who says what He means and means what He says. He should never be treated as a buddy who cannot be taken seriously; He is far too holy and powerful for that.

Second, you must have an unadulterated love for the Lord. Jesus said, "If anyone loves me, he will obey my teaching....He who does not love me will not obey my teaching" (John 14:23-24 NIV). John the beloved disciple wrote, "The man who says, 'I know him,' but does not do what he commands is a liar, and the truth is not in him. But if anyone obeys his word, God's love is truly made complete in him. This is how we know we are in him: Whoever claims to live in him must walk as Jesus did" (1 John 2:4-6 NIV).

Third, you must trust the Lord explicitly, even in the moments when it's hard to see past the current circumstances. Job said, "Though he slay me, yet will I trust in him: but I will maintain mine own ways before him" (Job 13:15 KJV).

Fourth, you must have a sense of destiny—a goal, a mission, something to hold out for: "Jesus...who for the joy that was set before him endured the cross, despising the shame…" (Hebrews 12:2 KJV). You must consider the end result, weigh the consequences realistically, and make a wise decision—one that might not be as much fun as indulging in the opportunity set before you, but will ultimately be for your own good. "He who gets wisdom loves his own soul; he who keeps understanding will find good" (Proverbs 19:8 NKJV). "Through wisdom a house is built, and by understanding it is established; by knowledge the rooms are filled with all precious and pleasant riches….So shall the knowledge of wisdom be to your soul; if you have found it, there is a prospect, and your hope will not be cut off" (Proverbs 24:3-4,14 NKJV).

And last, but certainly not least, remain transparent with God as well as a circle of loved ones who will speak the truth in love to you. Remain accountable at all costs to the saving of your own soul. Condemnation loves to make you hide your sin in a dark corner and then bury you in your mistakes. But Liberation comes as we expose ourselves to those who can lift us up while washing us with the Word of God. "Let us not give up meeting together, as some are in the habit of doing, but let us encourage one another—and all the more as you see the [Last] Day approaching" (Hebrews 10:25 NIV). We need to encourage one another to stay on the path.

In the Pit of Indecision

So what's your motivation for refusing that juicy carrot that Temptation is dangling in front of your nose? What should make you say no when everything inside of you screams, "Yes, yes, yes!"? Well, as I said earlier, good old fear has been known to give sense to many a fool. I recall when I was in school I had the reputation of being a "Miss Goody Two-Shoes." It certainly wasn't because the grand schemes my friends came up with didn't intrigue me. It was more out of a good old healthy dose of being afraid of what would happen to me once my mother found out about my latest shenanigans. I mean, *nothing* slipped by this woman! I came to the conclusion she had eyes in the back of her head—*and* an extra invisible pair that rolled out of her head and followed me wherever I went once I left the house. I could never understand how she knew everything that happened when she wasn't even there. It was downright uncanny. Something would happen at school, and she would know about it before I got home. You know the Scripture that says, "For the eyes of the LORD run to and fro throughout the whole earth..." (2 Chronicles 16:9 KJV)? That was my mother. I was afraid. Afraid of being confronted by her. Afraid of being spanked. Afraid of whatever awful punishment she would concoct to make me think twice about repeating my offense. As I grew older, however, I didn't join my friends in many of the things that they did because of the words of wisdom my mother and father spoke to me. Their instruction was engraved on my soul and in my mind. Whenever a questionable situation loomed before me, a tape would go on in my head that played my mother's and father's opinions on the subject. I then began basing my choices on the fact that, through the years, I'd learned that my parents had been right about most of the things they'd told me. So I moved past fear to trusting my parents' instruction to be sound. Unlike many teenagers, I did not feel that my parents hated me and didn't want me to have a good time. I knew that they loved me and wanted the best for me at all times. I also knew that the boundaries they had set for my life were their way of protecting me. Sometimes I felt that they were a bit overprotective, but I understood their motives.

But I even graduated past that reasoning to the point where I began to make decisions based solely on my love for my parents. I didn't want to do anything that would bring disappointment to their hearts. I knew that I was a reflection of my parents, and I always wanted people to give them a good report of their encounters with me. I wanted them to be proud of me.

And so it should be in our relationship with God. We must move from fear to faith, to love in our interaction with God in order to have any stability in our Christian walk. Let's face it—most of us came to God out of fear. Some of us wanted to avoid the fire-and-brimstone eternity the preacher was talking about. Some of us were in some pretty scary and desperate situations, and we decided that only God Himself could fix the mess we were in. Some of us just had a fear of the unknown and felt the need to settle accounts. Whatever the reason, fear is not ever going to be enough to carry you through the long haul of living the Christian life when Temptation comes to visit.

From Fear to Faith to Love

Yes, it is true that the fear of the Lord is the beginning of wisdom. Most of us walk away with two key words lodged in our brain cells—*fear* and *wisdom*. But the Word says the fear of the Lord is only the *beginning* of wisdom. If, with our getting of wisdom, we're also supposed to be getting understanding, exactly what is it that we are to understand? I believe we are supposed to understand the very character and heart of God. Only then can we move on to the next level of relationship with Him—trust.

"Trust in the LORD, and do good; [then you will] dwell in the land, and enjoy safe pasture" (Psalms 37:3 NIV). Interesting that the prerequisite for doing good is trusting God. But let's back up a few more verses to see what led David to come to this conclusion. He started off the psalm by saying, "Do not fret because of evil men or be envious of those who do wrong; for like the grass they will soon wither, like green plants they will soon die away" (verses 1-2 NIV). What are you saying, David? Do you mean that even *you* have had those days when you looked out and thought to yourself the same thing we often think? Thoughts like, *Everyone else in the world is doing whatever they feel like doing and getting away with it. Why am I killing myself trying to live a holy life? At the end of the day, what difference will it make? As a matter of fact, those who are doing their own thing seem to be prospering and doing a whole lot better than the ones who are dotting their spiritual i's and crossing their sanctified t's.*

What makes you press past that type of thinking? Simple childlike trust that God has your best interest at heart, even in the midst of seeming denial. In order to be healthy, this trust must have two sides. There is the side that knows that Abba Daddy is going to take care of everything. But there also has to be the side that knows He means what He says and says what He means.

I recall an incident that happened when I was a little girl which taught me a painful lesson. It happened shortly after one Christmas, when my dad was taking down the Christmas tree in the living room. I had friends playing with me in my room when my father called me to come to the living room. I had received a candy cane from Santa Claus and had hung it on the tree. My dad was now dismantling the tree, so he wanted me to come and get my candy cane. I yelled that I was coming, but continued playing. Dad called again. Once again I told him I was coming and continued my game. Finally he said, "If you don't come and get this thing right now, I'm going to give it to Sheila because obviously you don't want it. I'm not going to call you again."

Well, I didn't believe my dad would go that far. He knew that the candy cane was from my first encounter with Santa Claus and that it was a precious memento. But sure enough, after another five minutes had passed, he called Sheila to come and get the candy cane. I was horrified. I cried, I yelled, I tried to wrench the candy cane from Sheila's hand—all to no avail. Sheila was ushered from the house, candy cane in hand, while I was sent to my room to finish my tantrum alone. The lesson? Daddy means what he says.

This is where we get in trouble taking grace for granted. Like Samson, we find ourselves thinking that God is going to bail us out of yet another mess we've willfully and repeatedly committed, only to find that this time He's decided it's time for us to learn our lesson the hard way. I thought it was so cruel of my dad to give away my candy cane. After all, he knew how much it meant to me. But he knew something far more important. He knew I had to learn obedience. A candy cane was a small thing to sacrifice in order to gain the greater thing—a respect for the voice of my father. Listening to that voice without hesitation or question could someday save my life.

"He [God] chastises [corrects and disciplines] every son that He acknowledges, you must submit to discipline for He is doing what any loving father does for his children, no true son ever grows up uncorrected by his father. If you receive no correction, that discipline by which every man is trained, then it means that you aren't really God's son at all—that you don't really belong in His family. Besides this, our earthly fathers used to discipline us and we treated them with respect. Can we not more willingly subject ourselves to our spiritual Father? Our earthly fathers trained us for a few brief years, doing the best for us that they knew how, but God's correction is always right and for our best good, to enable us to share His holiness. Naturally all discipline seems hard to take at the time, it is in fact most unpleasant. Yet when it is all over we can see that its fruit is seen in the peacefulness of a righteous life" (Hebrews 12:7-11).[14]

Remember, all that God allows in our lives ultimately nudges us toward the place where we're in the position to be blessed. God wants to bless us! He wants us to live victorious lives filled with righteousness (right-standing with Him),

peace, and joy. The other side of trusting God is the comfort
of knowing that "there is a reward for the righteous" (Psalm
58:11 KJV). You and I must trust that there is a blessing in
store for us if we submit to our heavenly Father's commandments, irregardless of how much fun everyone else around us
seems to be having in the midst of disobedience. God is not
some terrestrial ogre sitting in the heavenlies, waiting to hit us
over the head with a baseball bat every time we miss the
mark. He is a loving Father who seeks to protect His children
from hurting themselves and being eternally lost. He is a
Father who would give anything for the sake of His children—including the life of His own Son. Which brings me to
the next level—love.

Love will make you do right even when you want to do
wrong. Love will make you change everything from your per-
sonality to the color of your hair. Love makes people do some
strange things. And that's the stuff we do when we're in love
with a human being who has limited resources and abilities.
When it comes to being able to respond in love to an all-
knowing, all-powerful, all-encompassing God, we seem to be
a little reluctant. Paul urges us to "present [our] bodies as a
living sacrifice, holy, acceptable to God, which is [our] *reasonable* service" (Romans 12:1 NKJV, emphasis added) after all
that He has done for us. Unfortunately, the trouble with a
living sacrifice is that it keeps crawling off the altar. But love
will make you stay there. Love makes a good woman stay
with a bad man. How much more should love cause us to cel-
ebrate a gracious God who crowns us with tender mercies
and generous care? How much more should our love for God
keep us from falling prey to the flirtations of Temptation?

When Love Makes the Difference

I must admit that there have been times in my life, especially early on in my walk with the Lord, when I had to confess

that I loved the temptation before me more than I loved God. The saving grace for me, I believe, was my honesty. I told God that He needed to increase my love for Him in order for me to walk away from those things that I knew would grieve His heart. He honored that prayer whenever I prayed it. I found that as my level of love was heightened, my desire for certain things took a nosedive. The things that looked so enticing before slowly lost their luster and appeal.

A Southern preacher once told his congregation, "Since I got saved I smoke as many cigarettes as I want, I party and run around with as many women as I want, I get as drunk as I want....The trouble is, I find I just don't want to." Love definitely changes your perspective on things. Your tastes change. You begin to love what the object of your affection loves and hate what they hate. It is the act of becoming one with another. When you're really in love with the Lord, He truly does give you the desires of your heart because you find that the things you crave become more and more a mirror of what He wants.

It is love that cries in the face of Temptation, "I refuse to grieve the heart of the Lover of my Soul by doing something that would offend Him." As Joseph stared into the eyes of a nameless, lustful woman recorded in biblical history only as Potiphar's wife, he must have struggled within. She must have been truly tempting. Satan doesn't waste his time enticing us with things we won't desire. So indeed Joseph was tempted. You can hear him rationalizing out loud as he told her, "Look...my master trusts me with everything in his entire household. No one here has more authority than I do! He has held back nothing from me except you, because you are his wife. How could I ever do such a wicked thing? It would be a great sin against God" (Genesis 39:8-9 NLT). Joseph cared what God thought. In spite of his difficult circumstances, where one would have been tempted to feel

forsaken by God, love won out over all. He still did not want
to offend His Lord.

When was the last time you decided not to do something
just because it would be a sin against God—even when you
didn't understand everything that was going on in your life?
Have you ever thought about the fact that, like Joseph, God
has entrusted you with authority and a vast array of things
that you can have access to? With that in mind, consider this:
The one thing He asks you not to touch should not feel like
a hardship or cruel denial.

The End of the Matter

Joseph not only developed a healthy fear, trust, and love
for the Lord, he went a step further—he considered the end
of the matter. You see, it is important to remember that Joseph
had a strong sense of purpose. His dream might not have
been absolutely clear to him at the time—or perhaps it was
clear, but had grown fuzzy during his years spent in slavery—
but he could not ignore the first call of his heart. This was
what kept him going when the enemy whispered in his ear,
"If you were in your own father's house, you would *have* servants instead of *being* a servant. You are entitled to more than
this. You don't have to keep up this humble act. You know it's
beneath you." Yet Joseph's sense of purpose, along with his
determination to see his destiny played out, caused him to
temper his attitude and work in expectancy toward the day
when his own greatness would be realized. His knowledge of
who God was and what He expected of His children caused
him to consider the end of momentary indulgences into sin.
The writings of the Jewish historian Josephus record this for
us:

> Neither did pity dissuade Joseph from his chastity, nor
> did fear (of her threatenings to falsely accuse him)
> compel him to a compliance with her; but he opposed

her solicitations, and did not yield to her threatenings,
and was afraid to do an ill thing, and chose to undergo
the sharpest punishment rather than to enjoy his present advantages, by doing what his own conscience
knew would justly deserve that he should die for it.

Joseph, according to Josephus, thought the entire scenario
over in great detail and continued his dissertation to try to
bring some reason to the mind of Mrs. Potiphar. He reminded
her that she was a married woman and that an affair would
simply "bring her to repentance afterwards, cause trouble to
her, and yet *would not amend what had been done amiss.*"
This is the part most of us overlook. Though God's forgiveness is faithful, the scars of sin remain—the pain of a broken
relationship, the remorse over an unwise purchase, the ruin
of a good reputation, the loss of a promising career, or an
irrevocable jail sentence. These things don't just fade away
once we repent. The fruit of our deeds remains to haunt us
and remind us of our errors.

But Joseph didn't stop there. He went on to have her consider "the fear she would be in lest they should be caught,
and that the *advantage of concealment was uncertain,* and
that only while the wickedness was not known would there
be any quiet for them." But listen to this! He tried to persuade
her that "she might have the enjoyment of her husband's
company without any danger, and he told her, that in the
company of her husband *she might have great boldness from
a good conscience,* both before God and before men." Boldness from a good conscience. What a refreshing thought!

And here's a statement that could be used in the work-
place today. He told her that she would "make use of her
authority over him better while she persisted in her chastity,
than when they were both ashamed for what wickedness
they had been guilty of, and that it is [this is my favorite line
out of this whole passage] *much better to depend on a good*

life, well acted, and known to have been so, than upon the hopes of the concealment of evil practices." Whew! What a guy! Small wonder God could set him up over Egypt next to the Pharaoh and trust him not to get a big head.

Now that is called considering the cost! Living in the fear of discovery can be more torturous than the actual exposure of our misdeeds. Joseph thought this thing out from beginning to end—what he had to gain, what he had to lose. A few moments of pleasure in exchange for his life didn't add up for him. Besides, hadn't God promised him something great? He seemed to have a recollection of a dream that prophetically outlined his future. Though things weren't looking very bright at present, something inside of him clung to that distant vision with undivided fervency.

Now, let's talk about another morsel Temptation had to have dangled before him—the temptation to become bitter.

First Joseph's own family sold him into slavery. Then God smiled on him and exalted him to head over the house in which he had been made a servant. Just as he got comfortable with accepting his lot in life and thinking things could be worse, the boss' wife started hitting on him—sexual harassment way back then. Truly, nothing *is* new under the sun. And then, to add insult to injury, he decided to do the right thing and ended up falsely accused and in jail. I mean, where is the justice in this life? This would have been way too much for the average man to handle. It makes a classic case for having an attitude. But Joseph persevered in maintaining a godly countenance.

A Matter of Trust

And you know why? Josephus states the reason profoundly: "Now Joseph, *commending all his affairs* to God, did not betake himself to make his defense, nor to give an account of the exact circumstances of the fact, but silently underwent the bonds and the distress he was in, *firmly believing that God, who knew the cause of his affliction and the truth of the fact, would be more powerful than those that inflicted the punishments upon him.*" Wow! Now that is what I call trusting God! Joseph trusted God when others would have accused God of abandoning them, of not intervening in their situation.

So how do we develop that kind of trust in God? David had a similar trust in God. When faced with the opportunity to kill Saul and get the guy off his back once and for all, David resisted the temptation to take matters into his own hands. Instead, he trusted God to deliver him from the hand of Saul and establish him as king. He called out to Saul and said, "Some urged me to kill you, but I spared you; I said, 'I will not lift my hand against my master, because he is the LORD's anointed.'...Now understand and recognize that I am not guilty of wrongdoing or rebellion. I have not wronged you, but you are hunting me down to take my life. May the LORD judge between you and me. And may the LORD avenge the wrongs you have done to me, but my hand will not touch you. As the old saying goes, 'From evildoers come evil deeds,' so my hand will not touch you....May the LORD be our judge and decide between us. May he consider my cause and uphold it; may he vindicate me by delivering me from your hand" (1 Samuel 24:10-13,15 NIV).

How could David trust God so implicitly? After all, God allowed Saul to hunt him like an animal for years. Why trust Him to save his life? Because David had that clean conscience that Joseph was talking about. Joseph and David had learned a secret that was the key to overcoming temptation. They had both moved past fear and faith to an unwavering love for the God they served. Though nothing is mentioned about Joseph's prayer life, I believe he was a praying man. He had to be, in order to possess the type of fruit that was so

evident in his life. The circumstances of his life were excru-
ciating. No one could bear up under the things that he
endured with so much grace unless they were completely
plugged into God and the leading of His Spirit.

Mike Murdock stated in one of his books something that
I've come to hide in my heart: "Isolation is necessary for intimacy, intimacy is necessary for impartation, and impartation
is necessary for change." Well, Joseph was isolated—taken
by force to a foreign country, surrounded by people who
spoke a language he didn't understand. Who did he really
have to talk to but God? I'm sure Joseph and God became
the best of friends in Joseph's early days of slavery. His relationship with God became his lifeblood. It was the thing that
sustained him and kept him from blowing a fuse when Mrs.
Potiphar, smarting from her spurned advances, chose to
falsely accuse him. Joseph clung to the hand of God as he
descended into jail and waited to see God move on his
behalf. This is difficult. While we wait for God to move, and
God waits for just the right time to turn His hand up, Temptation also waits for the first sigh of doubt to escape from our
lips. That's when Temptation moves into action—offering
alternatives and solutions to our situations that are merely
Band-Aids.

Band-Aids are interesting things. Initially they protect a
wound, but it's not healthy to keep the Band-Aid on too long
because a wound needs air in order to heal. And so it is with
us in the development of our souls. Sometimes I believe God
waits because our spirits need air—air to flex our trust muscles
and build up our faith. It is a process that cannot be short-
ened. For everyone who has ever tried to shorten the wait
and take matters into their own hands, they've produced an
Ishmael and have had to live with it. But those who sit tight
find, as Paul did, that "suffering produces perseverance; perseverance, character; and character, hope. And hope does not

disappoint us, because God has poured out his love into our hearts by the Holy Spirit, whom he has given us" (Romans 5:3-5 NIV). Another translation says, "For we know that trouble works fortitude, or produces endurance, and endurance strength of character, and our hope cannot shame us in the day of trial since God's love floods our hearts through the Holy Spirit which has been given to us."[15] Perhaps this is why the enemy of our soul comes bearing questions. If he can throw us off-balance and move us off the mark early in the game, then he can short-circuit the whole process that guarantees our victory.

Perhaps this is why God advises us that "in returning and rest shall ye be saved; in quietness and in confidence shall be your strength" (Isaiah 30:15 KJV). Return to the bosom of the Father and rest in His promises. Don't have conversations with the enemy. Remain quiet in the face of questions that rock the foundation of your faith. Stand in the confidence that God will perfect all things concerning you. This is when God's hands are released to do His best work on our behalf. Until then we are simply in the way, holding up our own progress.

We know from the psalms that not only was David a man of prayer, he was also a worshiper. He learned how to usher in the presence of God to keep him company because he, too, was isolated—first in the fields watching over his father's sheep, then on the run for years, hiding from a schizophrenic, paranoid king. Something happens when you spend quality time in the presence of God. Your perspective changes. Joseph changed from a spoiled brat who talked too much to a mature man who knew when to speak and when to hold his peace. The completion of this transformation ushered him into a place of incredible promotion. David changed from a naïve, impulsive young man with a natural sense of boldness into a king totally surrendered to his sovereign Lord. Both men yielded to the hand that would break them and then make them great and powerful men. They became men that God could trust with power because their hearts were now shaped like His.

This is the design God has for each of our lives. This is the design Temptation seeks to destroy. As each of us waits our turn in line for the desires of our hearts to be fulfilled, feeling somewhat in limbo between the pit and the palace, the temptation to ask, "Where is the reward in denial?" is overwhelming. This is when the call to "deny [yourself], and take up [your] cross daily, and follow me" (Luke 9:23 KJV) sounds cruel, unfeeling, and downright unsympathetic. Yet these actions are the very foundation of overcoming. This is where loving God becomes crucial. This is the love that dares to hope, dares to trust, dares to believe that, in spite of all you see and experience, God will arise on your behalf!

Love cries out in times of doubt, "But O my soul, don't be discouraged. Don't be upset. Expect God to act! For I know that I shall again have plenty of reason to praise him for all that he will do. He is my help! He is my God!"[16] (Psalm 42:11).

When Temptation calls, He is your help; He is your God.

11

THE REWARD OF DENIAL

"I know thy works: behold, I have set before thee an open door, and no man can shut it: for thou hast a little strength, and hast kept my word."

REVELATION 3:8 KJV

AND SO THE STORY GOES THAT JOSEPH was sold as a slave: "They bruised his feet with shackles, his neck was put in irons, till what he foretold came to pass, till the word of the LORD proved him true" (Psalm 105:18-19 NIV). Those who are destined for greatness become prime targets for Temptation. I can always tell when a great blessing or promotion is headed my way. The swirl of activity around me increases until all of my senses are literally reeling. I feel pulled and buffeted on every side. Now that I have become familiar with this pattern, I have learned to sit tight and make no impulsive moves. As the saying goes, "Higher levels, bigger devils." There is something to be said for maturing as we take this walk with Jesus.

Daniel proved that denying the flesh definitely worked to one's advantage. He was taken captive in the land of Babylon and ensconced in the king's palace along with his friends Hananiah, Mishael, and Azariah. They were later renamed Belteshazzar, Shadrach, Meshach, and Abednego, in respective order, to assimilate them into Babylonian society, I suppose. But I believe their renaming had an even deeper purpose. I believe the king of Babylon understood the significance of a name and sought to rearrange these young men spiritually, beginning with their outer identity—namely, their names.

What's in a Name?

It's interesting to further look at the names of these four men of God. *Daniel,* meaning "God is my Judge," was changed to *Belteshazzar,* which means "Bel protect his life!" (Bel was the chief Babylonian god.) *Hananiah,* meaning "the Lord shows grace," was changed to *Shadrach,* which means "under the command of Aku." (Aku was the moon god.) *Mishael,* meaning "Who is like God?" was changed to *Meshach,* which means "who is as Aku." *Azariah,* meaning "the Lord helps," was changed to *Abednego,* which means "servant of Nebo." (Nebo was the god of science and literature.) And so each man was renamed to superimpose the spiritual beliefs of the Babylonians over their Jewish foundational understanding of the God of Abraham, Isaac, and Jacob. But Daniel clung to his original name with ferocity.

I find it rather intriguing that every time Daniel is mentioned in the book of Daniel, it always says, "and Daniel, whose name *was* Belteshazzar." Even Nebuchadnezzar himself referred to him by his original name. This continues up to the fifth chapter of Daniel, and then it seems as if everyone must have gotten tired of the whole name business because he was simply referred to as "Daniel" after that. And the bottom line is that the book is called the book of Daniel, not the book of Belteshazzar.

Not only did Daniel refuse to acknowledge his name change, he also made the decision not to sample the tidbits of compromise that Temptation so smoothly offered. This is commendable under the circumstances. Here Daniel and his friends are carried away captive to a strange land. Their plight could have been a bitter one of forced labor, but instead they were taken to the king's palace to be trained and fattened up for the king's service. It reminds me of the story of Hansel and Gretel. Remember how the witch purposed to fatten up the two children in order to eat them? Sometimes it's good for us to keep in mind that Satan will attempt to entice us with mouth-watering delicacies; however, he has a darker end in mind than your typical gourmet cook, who merely enjoys watching others partake of his concoctions with delight.

So Daniel and his friends were ushered into the king's courts: "The King assigned them a daily amount of food and wine from the king's table. They were to be trained for three years, and after that they were to enter the king's service" (Daniel 1:5 NIV). But the Bible says that "Daniel resolved not to defile himself with the royal food and wine, and he asked the chief official for permission not to defile himself this way....Daniel then said to the guard whom the chief official had appointed over Daniel, Hananiah, Mishael and Azariah, 'Please test your servants for ten days: Give us nothing but vegetables to eat and water to drink. Then compare our appearance with that of the young men who eat the royal food, and treat your servants in accordance with what you see.' So he agreed to this and tested them for ten days. At the end of the ten days they looked healthier and better nourished than any of the young men who ate the royal food. So the guard took away their choice food and the wine they were to drink and gave them vegetables instead.

"To these four young men God gave knowledge and under-standing of all kinds of literature and learning. And Daniel could understand visions and dreams of all kinds. At the end of the time set by the king to bring them in, the chief official presented them to Nebuchadnezzar. The king talked with them, and he found none equal to Daniel, Hananiah, Mishael and Azariah. *In every matter of wisdom and understanding about which the king questioned them, he found them ten times better than all the magicians and enchanters in his whole kingdom"* (Daniel 1:8,11-20 NIV, emphasis added).

Though Daniel was *in* the Babylonian world, he certainly had no plans to be *of* it. Most in his situation would have rel-ished the idea of having food from the king's table at their disposal. They would have found this a delight and a privi-lege, and would have dove in headfirst, taking full advantage of the spread. But Daniel had the end of the matter in mind. And truly, the end justified his request. Daniel and his three friends, who also chose not to sample the tidbits of compro-mise, looked and functioned better than those who indulged themselves. Not only were Daniel and his friends in better health than the others, but they were also intellectually and spiritually sharper. God blessed them with supernatural intel-ligence and made them highly sensitive in the Spirit. Because of this they were promoted into the king's service and went on to enjoy political prominence.

Watch What You Eat

"Eating well," I believe, is God's will for His children today. But when will we learn that Christians cannot eat what the world eats? I'm not talking about just food here. We cannot eat the world's standards and opinions. We cannot sit and digest the same diet of garbage that the world practically inhales on a daily basis via television, radio, and question-able conversations held by the office water cooler. You know what I'm talking about. We take in all of the news and the talk shows and the sitcoms and the movies. We listen to all of the world's lyrics that assault us over the airwaves, and then we run to a friend and say, "Did you see that show that was on last night where this happened?" or, "Did you hear that song about so-and-so?" And even though we're shocked by the content, we continue repeating it in our displeasure or downright laughing in incredulity. And by so doing, we defile our inner man.

These things of the world enter through our eyes and ears, lodge in our hearts, and come back out of our mouths. Once repeated, they're filed in our minds, where they settle comfortably into our subconscious. And each of these things waits for the right moment to rise up and superimpose itself over a thought that has left a convenient space to accommodate it. The next step we take is to put that thought into action. This is what we do when we meditate. We begin to meditate on what the world is saying and doing, and it becomes a part of our conversation and defiles us. "Don't you see that whatever enters the mouth goes into the stomach and then out of the body? But the things that come out of the mouth come from the heart, and these make a man 'unclean'" (Matthew 15:17-18 NIV). To live in integrity, there must be a marriage of our own effort with God's help. David said in Psalm 101:3, "I will set before my eyes no vile thing. The deeds of faithless men I hate; they will not cling to me" (NIV). Daniel and David knew something we need to grasp with an even deeper conviction than we possess at present. We must be careful to guard the gates of our eyes, our ears, and our lips. We are absorbing more than we care to admit in the name of remaining well-informed. It was never God's plan that we judge evil through experiential knowledge. It was His intent that we discern it and avoid it, thus keeping ourselves free from its influence.

The world does a tantalizing dance, this we will admit. But we shouldn't be so naïve as to feel that we can stand on the fringes of the party without at least tapping our feet to the music. The rhythm eventually will snatch us up and carry us away. If we linger long enough, we'll find ourselves humming the tune that's playing under our breath without even realizing it. Daniel, deeming it more important to keep his wits about him, turned down his plate. Daniel crucified the flesh, choosing to put his body under subjection. Because he lived his life in such total obedience, he was able to believe that God had his back, and he walked with a boldness most of us would find difficult to master. He boldly spoke the truth to the Babylonian kings, telling them that, in God's eyes, their act was not together.

I'm sure all of the yes-men in the palace quaked in fear every time Daniel boldly proclaimed a "thus saith the Lord" message. Yet the more truth he spoke, the more he was revered and promoted. Which goes to prove that even if the world doesn't like what you're saying, they will respect you for standing your ground and speaking your heart. Daniel survived four different administrations as each king succeeding the throne continued to keep him at a high rank. It is written that "Daniel so distinguished himself among the administrators and the satraps by his exceptional qualities that the king planned to set him over the whole kingdom" (Daniel 6:3 NIV). Well, this so incensed the yes-men in the kingdom that they began to plot Daniel's demise. And what I find interesting is that they "tried to find grounds for charges against Daniel in his conduct of government affairs, but they were unable to do so. They could find no corruption in him, because he was trustworthy and neither corrupt nor negligent.

"Finally these men said, 'We will never find any basis for charges against this man Daniel unless it has something to do with the law of his God'" (Daniel 6:4-5 NIV). They then proceeded to manipulate the king into signing a decree that was to last thirty days—a decree that outlawed prayer to any god or man except the king. Anyone caught breaking the law would be thrown into the lions' den.

Can you believe that?! This is a classic example of how the enemy tries to find grounds for charges against us. It is the job of Temptation to lavish us with innumerable opportunities to fulfill the requirements for accusation. We, like Daniel, must purpose in our own hearts not to defile ourselves with the world's morsels. This way we, too, can be free from corruption when the accuser of the brethren comes stalking. The only way that Daniel's enemies could get to him was to force him to break a man-made law that overstepped the boundaries of his relationship with his God. That is a profound statement on the character of Daniel.

Standing Against the Odds

I wonder how many of us would have the courage to continue to pray openly after a life-threatening edict had been issued. Yet Daniel did not bow to Temptation by even *pretending* to compromise. He boldly continued the same habit he had maintained for years, praying three times a day in front of the windows in his home that faced Jerusalem. He was caught praying to God and was brought before the king to receive his punishment. And because the law could not be revoked, all the king could do was throw up his hands and say, "May your God, whom you serve continually, rescue you!" (Daniel 6:16 NIV). And so Daniel was thrown to the lions. After a tense and sleepless night, the king made his way to the lions' den, where he heard an unharmed Daniel proclaim, "O king, live forever! My God sent his angel, and he shut the mouths of the lions. They have not hurt me, *because I was found innocent in his sight.* Nor have I ever done any wrong before you, O king" (verse 21, emphasis added). On that note, Daniel was lifted from the lions' den, and no wound was found on him because he had trusted his God (see verse 23). But the story doesn't end there, and it's important to note what happened next: "At the king's command, the men who had falsely accused Daniel were brought in and thrown into the lions' den, along with their wives and children. And before they reached the floor of the den, the lions overpowered them and crushed all their bones. Then King Darius wrote to all the peoples, nations and men of every language throughout the land: 'May you prosper greatly! I issue a decree that in every part of my kingdom people must fear and reverence the God of Daniel. For he is the living God and he endures forever; his kingdom will not be destroyed, his dominion will never end. He rescues and he saves; he performs signs and wonders in the heavens and on the earth. He has rescued Daniel from the power of the lions.' So Daniel prospered during the reign of Darius and the reign of Cyrus the Persian" (verses 24-28).

There is a boldness that comes from a clear conscience that takes us to another dimension of faith. It is the place of miracles, the place where God shows Himself strong on your behalf. Truly, "when a man's ways are pleasing to the LORD, he makes even his enemies live at peace with him" (Proverbs 16:7 NIV). I'm sure the administrators and satraps who plotted Daniel's ruin never counted on God's intervention or the backlash of their own manipulations. They didn't know who they were dealing with!

Nor did Nebuchadnezzar know who he was dealing with when he constructed an image of gold and commanded all to bow down and worship it. Bow down and worship with musical accompaniment, no less! This makes me pause and wonder what is really happening today with celebrity worship at an all-time high. Just think of the extreme emotions that take place at popular music concerts—the tears, the screaming, the fainting spells, the violence, the drug abuse, the chanting, the complete abandon that overtakes the audience—it is scary when you view it in this context.

Yet Shadrach, Meshach, and Abednego, who were not moved by any menacing threats about being thrown into a fiery furnace, told Temptation to pack up his little snacks of compromise and get lost. When confronted by the king about their disobedience to his command, they boldly stood their ground and said, "'O Nebuchadnezzar, we do not need to defend ourselves before you in this matter. If we are thrown into the blazing furnace, the God we serve is able to save us from it, and he will rescue us from your hand, O king. *But even if he does not, we want you to know, O king, that we will not serve your gods or worship the image of gold you have set up*'" (Daniel 3:16-18 NIV, emphasis added). Well, you just gotta love them for that comment: "Even if he does not, we want you to know that we will not serve your gods." But the king was not amused. He had the furnace heated seven times hotter than its original temperature. It was now so hot that the soldiers who took Shadrach, Meschach, and Abednego to the furnace died from the heat.

Well, you know the rest of the story. But I'll tell it anyway, simply because I love it so much and it illustrates a point that I want to make. The book of Daniel says that the king jumped up in amazement because he saw four men walking unbound in the midst of the fire, and one looked like a son of the gods. So he approached the opening of the blazing furnace and shouted, "Shadrach, Meshach and Abednego, servants of the Most High God, come out! Come here!" (Daniel 3:26 NIV). So they came out and everyone crowded around them and were amazed to find "that the fire had not harmed their bodies, nor was a hair of their heads singed;

their robes were not scorched, and there was no smell of fire on them" (verse 27).

And do you know what Nebuchadnezzar said after this? He said, "'Praise be to the God of Shadrach, Meshach and Abednego, who has sent his angel and rescued his servants! *They trusted in him and defied the king's command and were willing to give up their lives* rather than serve or worship any god except their own God. Therefore I decree that the people of any nation or language who say anything against the God of Shadrach, Meshach and Abednego be cut into pieces and their houses be turned into piles of rubble, for no other god can save in this way.' Then the king promoted Shadrach, Meshach and Abednego in the province of Babylon" (verses 28-30, emphasis added).

I want you to see something here that is so subtle that it could easily be missed if you didn't take a second look. And it is important to notice because it is the very heart of Satan's concentration—*worship.* There's that word again. In both Daniel's and Shadrach, Meshach, and Abednego's refusal to compromise their worship, something very significant happened. Because they had clean consciences and were in right standing with God, He came to their aid in a miraculous way that was startlingly clear to those who were present. In turn, this manifestation of God's divine and supernatural protection caused those who had opposed the four men's stands to now glorify and worship their God.

Not only did the king now have to give homage where homage was due, but he issued an edict for the rest of the land to reverence this true and living God. That is powerful! What would happen if we could get to the point where we, too, drew back and chose not to yield to Temptation's promise of an easy life in exchange for not rocking the boat, or partaking in a harmless little compromise in order to keep the peace, or going along with the program so others won't view us as fanatical Christians?

The world would be changed if we chose to walk as these four walked—with immovable faith and clear consciences. Faith that inspired God to arise and perform. Consciences that encouraged God to glorify Himself in our midst and draw others to recognize His majesty. In contrast, our disobedience stifles the movement of God. Disobedience paves the way for Him to be robbed of praise as the world scoffs at the fall of yet another Christian, sneering at the "humanness" of yet another saint caught in the throes of what the unsaved view as failure to uphold godly standards. God is robbed of praise while Satan and Temptation smile and shake hands… mission accomplished.

They are pleased to present their accusations of our failure to God, reminding Him that, on the grounds of His own Word, He cannot promote us. Many say that our heavenly Father should have mercy. Well, that's exactly what He has. He knows that it is not merciful to reinforce bad behavior with undeserved rewards. Mercy knows that you don't give children what they cannot handle lest they hurt themselves. Promotion placed in the hands of one who compromises to save his own skin can be a dangerous thing. This is the same person who would sell out a nation if he were faced with the right circumstances, or end his own career in disgrace because compromise so easily transitions into blatant dishonesty. God's grace and mercy will not allow Him to propel any of His children toward this end.

Anytime we choose to take our lives into our own hands— and that is what compromise actually is—God steps aside. When we manipulate our circumstances to gain comfort or access to our own desires instead of allowing God to move on our behalf, we rob Him of an opportunity to manifest His glory. Why? Because we're too busy being our own gods, too busy positioning ourselves to gain our own desires, our own favors, our own accolades, our own glory, so to speak. And we ought to know by now that God has said, "I will not give my glory to another or my praise to idols" (see Isaiah 42:8). God's mercy protects us from our worst enemy—ourselves. Therefore, we all should seek to arrive at a place of maturity where we can truly release our wills into God's care and "let God be God in our lives." We are able to do this when we are willing to accept that God's prevention is not a form of robbery, but a mechanism of divine protection.

The Final Curtain

Consider the end of the lives we've examined so far and notice the differences. Let's begin with a comparison between Daniel, who ended his life in peace and honor because of his refusal to eat what the world was serving, and Solomon, whose indulgences in worldly fare—namely, foreign women—cost him in the end. The Bible says that "the LORD became angry with Solomon because his heart had turned away from the LORD, the God of Israel, who had appeared to him twice. Although he had forbidden Solomon to follow other gods, Solomon did not keep the LORD's command" (verses 9-10). The only thing that saved Solomon was a promise that God had made to David. He promised David the legacy of his house, his kingdom, and his throne being established forever (see 2 Samuel 7:16). Even in the face of Solomon's adamant disobedience when it came to marrying foreign women, God refused to break His promise to David.

Though God was furious with Solomon for turning to the gods of his foreign wives, He told him, "Since...you have not kept my covenant and my decrees, which I commanded you, I will most certainly tear the kingdom away from you and give it to one of your subordinates. Nevertheless, for the sake of David your father, I will not do it during your lifetime. I will tear it out of the hand of your son. Yet I will not tear the whole kingdom from him, but will give him one tribe for the sake of David my servant and for the sake of Jerusalem, which I have chosen" (1 Kings 11:11-13 NIV).

Talk about the strength of a covenant! I wonder what would have happened if God hadn't promised David anything. But one has to wonder how happy Solomon was in his final days. The Lord raised up enemies against him, rebellion broke out, and Solomon made the rather sad summation in the book of Ecclesiastes that "all was vanity." His son Rehoboam, who succeeded him as king, promptly began his reign by foolishly angering the tribes of Israel. Rehoboam was able to retain only two tribes under his rule—the house of Judah and the tribe of Benjamin. This began the era of the split kingdoms, which eventually led to complete upheaval and captivity. Not exactly the type of legacy David or Solomon had in mind, I would surmise. But, once again, Temptation had dealt Solomon a hand that, despite his wisdom, he couldn't resist. The bottom line remains: "No one can serve two masters. Either he will hate the one and love the other, or he will be devoted to the one and despise the other" (Matthew 6:24 NIV). This passage applies to more than money; it holds true for anything in our lives that diverts our focus from the lordship of God in our lives.

But God's plan was greater than Temptation's manipulations, and even as He handed a portion of the kingdom over to Jeroboam, He told him—in Michelle paraphrase—"Look, I cannot blink at Solomon's disobedience, neither can I break my promise to David. So here's what I'm gonna do. I'm going to give you ten tribes and give one tribe to Solomon's son so that my servant David will always have a lamp before me in Jerusalem. Now, if you will be obedient to me, I will build you a dynasty just as fabulous as David's and give you Israel. I will humble David's descendants because of their disobedience, but don't get too happy, because this will not last forever" (1 Kings 11:34-39). God has never allowed man's sin to interrupt His plans. To the great disgruntlement of Satan, no one's time gets wasted. Each person involved in the scheme of God's sovereign plan gets to learn valuable lessons if they choose to do so.

And that leads me to my next point: Samson died amidst the rubble of his own bad choices. But at least he finally got it! He finally came to the place where he realized that he could only do all things through the strengthening power of the Lord Almighty Himself. Samson's weakness was turned to strength as he humbled himself before God and prayed one last prayer: "O Sovereign LORD, remember me. O God, please strengthen me just once more, and let me with one blow get revenge on the Philistines for my two eyes" (Judges 16:28 NIV). God gave Samson exactly what he prayed for. In one last blaze of victorious glory that earned him a place in the hall of fame with those of great faith, he leveled the temple where the Philistines were gathered, killing more of them that day than he had throughout his *entire* life.

I sometimes wonder what would have happened if Samson had prayed a different prayer. Something like, "Lord, please make a way of escape for me, and let me be more effective this time around now that I know better." But perhaps the handicap of being blind would have been something he couldn't survive. Or perhaps he knew his own weaknesses better than we think he did and thought it best to make a clean exit. Who can say? Yet I am always saddened as I ponder his biography. I feel that Samson died prematurely. Yes, it was prophesied that he would "begin the deliverance of Israel from the hands of the Philistines" (Judges 13:5 NIV). But think of what a glorious thing it would have been to have had Samson around for awhile—marrying the right woman, having sons who grew up to inherit his anointing and carry on his tradition of defeating the enemies of the Lord with supernatural strength, and leaving a rich legacy of victories for his children's children to share...like Joseph did! In contrast, think about the end of Joseph's life. Joseph "lived a hundred and ten years and saw the third generation of Ephraim's children. Also the children of Makir son of Manasseh were placed at birth on Joseph's knees....And Joseph made the sons of Israel swear an oath and said, 'God will surely come to your aid, and then you must carry my bones up from this place.' So Joseph died at the age of a hundred and ten. And after they embalmed him, he was placed in a coffin in Egypt" (Genesis 50:22-23,25-26 NIV). What a long, full, rich life. Joseph ended his life in peace, surrounded by his children and his children's children. Later, as the Israelites left Egypt, his descendants kept his request and carried his bones with them, burying them in the Promised Land.

What was the difference between Joseph and Samson? The excuse of being victims of circumstance isn't sound enough as we ponder the fate of these two men who had similar beginnings. Both were miracle babies in a sense. Remember? Rachel, Joseph's mother, was barren. So distraught was Rachel that she told her husband, Jacob, "Give me children, or else I die" (Genesis 30:1 KJV). Rachel's story is an ironic study in itself, seeing that she later died in childbirth while having her second son. I believe that sometimes the things we think we will die without are the main things that God knows will kill us. In His protective grace, He withholds these things from us. In exchange, He suffers much abuse from our bad attitudes as we whine and murmur in our lack of understanding and trust in His decisions. But that's a whole other ball of wax! Anyway, miracle baby Joseph was highly favored by his parents to the point of stirring up the jealousy of his other siblings.

Samson was a miracle child also. His parents were well along in age when an angel appeared to them, bearing news that they would have a son who would be set apart by God as a deliverer of the people. So we can surmise that both of these little boys were spoiled. That is a given, considering the qualifying factors. They were brought up with the same set of values. Both of them had parents who worshiped God and lived in accordance with His laws, yet something happened to separate them along the way. Both Joseph and Samson had an encounter with a woman, and this is where they went their separate ways—inwardly, that is. Outwardly, they both landed in jail as a result of their encounters. So what *was* the difference between them? The difference was in the way they handled their encounters—in the *how* and the *why*. You see, Joseph had a dream he couldn't forget, while Samson had a purpose he never really embraced. This is the root of all of the fruit that came to bear in these two men's lives. While Joseph fled from sin, Samson became comfortable in it. While Samson retaliated against his enemies, further incensing them against him, Joseph endured abuse, forgave his enemies, and was promoted. God caused Joseph to forget all his trouble and all his father's household (see Genesis 41:51), but stirred Samson to remember from whence he came. Joseph became fruitful in the land of his affliction (see Genesis 41:52), while Samson became blind in order to see. Similar beginnings, drastically different ends. The deciding factor? Yielding to the desires of the flesh. Joseph understood that there were consequences to be suffered for every wrong action. He also realized that if God was who He said He was, then surely He rewarded the righteous for their obedience. Samson's thought process did not venture beyond the immediate gratification of the flesh. For him, there was only today. A preacher once said, "We are all one decision away from disaster." Temptation knows that, he counts on it, and he times his appearances well.

A Tale of Two Kings

And what of the two shy guys who became mighty kings? Again, another study in contrasts—Saul and David. Saul began his reign as a tall, strikingly handsome king. He was the people's choice, yet he ended up lowered to the rungs of paranoid and schizophrenic behavior. He literally fell on his own sword, committing suicide throughout his reign, as well as in the end. Saul died because he was unfaithful to the Lord; he did not keep the Word of the Lord and even consulted a medium for guidance, and did not inquire of the Lord. So the Lord put him to death and turned the kingdom over to David, the son of Jesse (see 1 Chronicles 10:13-14). What a sad and miserable end it was after such a commendable entry into prominence. On top of this, look what happened to the nation: "When the Israelites along the valley and those across the Jordan saw that the Israelite army had fled and that Saul and his sons had died, they abandoned their towns and fled. And the Philistines came and occupied them" (1 Samuel 31:7 NIV). Look at that! The enemy moved right in and took up gleeful residence. This is a good example of what happens when we abdicate our rightful place in the kingdom. And the disgrace didn't end there. The Philistines took Saul's body, stripped off his armor, cut off his head, and hung his body on a wall, giving credit to their gods for the victory. There's that worship thing again.

Now, let's cut to a scene years later. Here we see David resting upon his couch in the palace nearing the end of his life. He calls in his son Solomon to give him parting instructions. Then after telling Solomon how to deal with his enemies, "David rested with his fathers and was buried in the City of David. He had reigned forty years over Israel—seven years in

Hebron and thirty-three in Jerusalem. So Solomon sat on the throne of his father David, and his rule was firmly established" (1 Kings 2:10-11 NIV).

Not only did David leave Solomon with sound advice, he also left him with a secure throne in the midst of a country in peace. In addition, he also left the plans for the building of the temple along with all the materials that had been collected and were ready to be put to use. In short, David set Solomon up well: "A good man leaves an inheritance for his children's children" (Proverbs 13:22 NIV). So Saul died leaving the legacy of death to his sons, cutting off his name forever, while David left a rich legacy—spiritually as well as materially—to his son Solomon. What separated these two kings?

Well, even though Saul was quick to tell the prophet Samuel that he could not possibly be king because he was from the most insignificant tribe of Israel, he indeed had a privileged background. Handsome and striking, he had the perfect exterior package to be the king of Israel. David, however, was from a simple background, where he watched over the sheep in his father's field. Though he hailed from the tribe chosen to bear the lineage of Jesus Christ, David himself was the smallest and most insignificant member of his family. Yet while Saul had a fear of the people, David had a heart for God. Saul always had a justification for his disobedience to the Lord. But David...David knew how to repent. Both men fell into major sins, but the deciding factor that separated their destinies was David's ability to repent.

This is an option open to all of us as believers. The comfort in the myriad of all the wrong choices we make is that we have a heavenly Father who says, "Come now, and let us reason together.... Though your sins are like scarlet, they shall be as white as snow" (Isaiah 1:18 NKJV). But we must be willing to come clean with the One who is capable of cleansing us. So Saul, when confronted by the prophet of

God about his sin, cried—in Michelle paraphrase—"Hey, what did you expect me to do with all these people on my back? I had to give the people what they wanted!" While David simply threw up his hands and thought to himself, *Oh, well, there's no need for me to try to deny it. I have no excuse. I've sinned; let's call it what it is* (my paraphrase again). And David was not sad because he had been caught; he was sad because he knew that *he had hurt the heart of God.* That was the thing that burdened him. That's right; he got straight to the point: "I have sinned against the LORD." Short, sweet, simple, to the point. And Nathan the prophet replied, "The LORD has taken away your sin. You are not going to die" (2 Samuel 12:13 NIV).

Rising to the Occasion

After David's infant son, who was conceived in sin, died, "David got up from the ground. After he had washed, put on lotions and changed his clothes, he went into the house of the LORD and worshiped. Then he went to his own house, and at his request they served him food, and he ate. His servants asked him, 'Why are you acting this way? While the child was alive, you fasted and wept, but now that the child is dead, you get up and eat!' He answered, 'While the child was still alive, I fasted and wept. I thought, "Who knows? The LORD may be gracious to me and let the child live." But now that he is dead, why should I fast? Can I bring him back again? I will go to him, but he will not return to me.' Then David comforted his wife Bathsheba, and he went to her and lay with her. She gave birth to a son, and they named him Solomon" (2 Samuel 12:20-24 NIV). David also knew how to accept the punishment for his sins gracefully and move on. He understood that the chastening of the Lord was to teach him obedience. Yet many of us have created our own theology in which God, if He were truly merciful, would blot out all consequences. And what would we learn if we didn't find out that a hot stove really does burn? Even Jesus, "Though he were a Son, yet learned he obedience by the things which he suffered" (Hebrews 5:8 KJV).

The whole Bathsheba incident was not the last time David did something to displease God, but he never got a big head or arrived at a place where he didn't feel the need to answer to God because he was a king. As a matter of fact, David came to the place where he was so sensitive to the heart of God that he didn't have to be confronted by a prophet. The Bible says that "David was conscience-stricken after he had counted the fighting men, and he said to the LORD, 'I have sinned greatly in what I have done. Now, O LORD, I beg you, take away the guilt of your servant. I have done a very foolish thing'" (2 Samuel 24:10 NIV).

The prophet of the Lord was then sent to David to ask him to choose one of three punishments. David chose a plague that was to last for three days. "When David saw the angel who was striking down the people, he said to the LORD, 'I am the one who has sinned and done wrong. These are but sheep. What have they done? Let your hand fall upon me and my family'" (2 Samuel 24:17 NIV). So the prophet of the Lord instructed David to go and give a sacrifice to the Lord. The man who owned the threshing floor where David planned to make the sacrifice offered to give it to him for free, but David replied, "No, I insist on paying you for it. I will not sacrifice to the LORD my God burnt offerings that cost me nothing" (verse 24). After he made his sacrifice to the Lord, the Lord answered his prayer and stopped the plague. David not only knew how to repent, but he also knew how to take responsibility. That is all God asks for. He remembers that we are only human: "As a father has compassion on his children, so the LORD has compassion on those who fear him;

for he knows how we are formed, he remembers that we are dust" (Psalms 103:13-14 NIV).

With this train of thought in mind, God's promises toward David prevailed, in spite of his failings: "When your days are over and you rest with your fathers, I will raise up your offspring to succeed you, who will come from your own body, and I will establish his kingdom. He is the one who will build a house for my Name, and I will establish the throne of his kingdom forever. I will be his father, and he will be my son. When he does wrong, I will punish him with the rod of men, with floggings inflicted by men. But my love will never be taken away from him, as I took it away from Saul, whom I removed from before you. Your house and your kingdom will endure forever before me; your throne will be established forever" (2 Samuel 7:12-16 NIV).

The Ultimate Aim

While Temptation thrives on our failure, God is not surprised or overwhelmed by it. He understands that even a good man will struggle and fall. As a matter of fact, He knows the way we take even when we feel as Paul felt, "I do not understand what I do. For what I want to do I do not do, but what I hate I do" (Romans 7:15 NIV). We may have the best of intentions, but still we do wrong. "A just man falleth seven times, and riseth up again" (Proverbs 24:16 KJV). God knows and stands by us, willing to be our help. "The steps of a good man are ordered by the LORD: and he delighteth in his way. Though he fall, he shall not be utterly cast down: for the LORD upholdeth him with his hand" (Psalm 37:23-24 KJV).

Perhaps it is sometimes difficult to grasp that compassionate hand because of our own shame and disappointment at our failings. Even more difficult can be the ability to forgive ourselves. And so we continue to remind God of sins that He has thrown into the sea of forgetfulness. It is hard for us to believe that His compassion could be that complete. Small wonder Micah wondered aloud, "Where is another God like you, who pardons the sins of the survivors among his people? You cannot stay angry with your people forever, because you delight in showing mercy. Once again you will have compassion on us. You will trample our sins under your feet and throw them into the depths of the ocean!" (Micah 7:18-19 NLT). And God replies, "I—yes, I alone—am the one who blots out your sins for my own sake and will never think of them again. Let us review the situation together, and you can present your case if you have one" (Isaiah 43:25-26 NLT).

Willing to forgive? Yes, indeed! Willing to allow us to wallow in our sins? Absolutely not! So what is the turning point? How do we break the cycle of rising and falling in our own lives? Let's face it, sometimes even considering the end of the matter is not enough to stop us from salivating and eventually sneaking one little nibble from Temptation's plate. There is always a part of us that thinks we will be the first one to sidestep the consequences. It's not true, but we hope against hope, and end up chagrined when things work out differently. As we limp away with our backsides stinging from condemnation, we once again find ourselves wondering why we were so foolish to fall for Temptation's same old trick.

By now you should know "if you do sin, there is someone to plead for you before the Father. He is Jesus Christ, the one who pleases God completely" (1 John 2:1 NLT). But—in the interest of not trampling mud through the blood of Jesus repeatedly—what is the deciding factor that makes us, like Joseph, conclude that life is far more worth the living when one's conscience is clear? What causes us to have a conviction as strong as Daniel's, to adamantly refuse to defile ourselves with the world's spread? Not by performing mere religious service that brings no joy. Not by acting like the Christians in the Ephesian church, who went through the motions of Christianity but had lost their first love—the passion, the romance, of their relationship with God. What we need is the type of service that is wrought with a sincere and adoring heart—a heart like Mary, who chose the better part, indulging herself in her relationship with Jesus. Service and obedience without love become empty labors that are hard to maintain. What is the deciding factor when Temptation extends his hand? Our love for God—plain and simple.

We all must continually revisit the place of examining our love for the Lord when confronted with the things that Temptation sometimes dangles within our reach. We all must be willing to repent and admit, "Lord, I have to be honest with You. I just don't love You enough to release this thing. I need Your help. I need You to increase my love for You and my hatred for the things that are not pleasing to You." He will be faithful to meet you every time you've prayed that prayer. You see, you have His promise: "No temptation has seized you except what is common to man. And God is faithful; he will not let you be tempted beyond what you can bear. But when you are tempted, he will also provide a way out so that you can stand up under it" (1 Corinthians 10:13 NIV). It's true: "*Whoever calls upon the name of the LORD shall be saved*" (Romans 10:13 NKJV, emphasis added). That includes salvation from Temptation.

The question is this: Do you want to be saved from something that your flesh is screaming for? When Temptation seizes you and caresses you so deliciously, the deciding factor that determines whether or not you give in will be whether you are willing to break the heart of God for a momentary indulgence.

I remember that several years ago there was a book on the market entitled *Make Love Your Aim*. That about sums up what we're talking about here. I believe our aim should be to increase our love for God and secure our relationship with

Him instead of memorizing all the rules by rote. That is the true test, as far as God is concerned. "If someone says, 'I belong to God,' but doesn't obey God's commandments, that person is a liar and does not live in the truth. But those who obey God's word really do love him" (1 John 2:4-5 NLT).

If that isn't enough to convince you that love is the key to overcoming Temptation, ponder this: Jesus said, "'You must love the Lord your God with all your heart, all your soul, and all your mind.' This is the first and greatest commandment. A second is equally important: 'Love your neighbor as yourself.' All the other commandments and all the demands of the prophets are based on these two commandments" (Matthew 22:37-40 NLT). This simply means that if we truly love God, the thought of doing anything that He dislikes should be repulsive to us. The flesh is weak; therefore, whatever the heart says, goes. How do we turn away the plate that Temptation serves? By liking better what God is serving. The bottom line is perhaps too simple for the masses—being completely and totally in love with God. In other words, it all comes right back around to the very first point: true worship.

12

TO HIM WHO OVERCOMES

"Him that overcometh will I make a pillar in the
temple of my God, and he shall go no more out: and
I will write upon him the name of my God..."

REVELATION 3:12 KJV

ALTHOUGH THE REWARD OF DENIAL might not be immediately
apparent, believe me, the chickens do eventually come home
to roost. Tomorrow may not be promised, but for the majority
of people it still comes. And with it comes the harvest of what
was done, or not done, the day before. What was done yes-
terday definitely affects today, which will ultimately affect
tomorrow. There is no escaping this as fact. Whether we're
sorry or not, the result of words said and actions impulsively
enacted come to visit us in the form of reminders we usually
do not like.

We can go through all the arguments about being "only
human" and living in the "here and now." We have a million
reasons for following the mood of our flesh. But we must
keep in mind that if a reward is what we're after, the greater

reward lies in overcoming the urges of the heart. The immediate is actually a temporary state. This is the fine print that
Temptation doesn't allow us to read as he urges us to sign on
the dotted line. He is patient but unkind, waiting until we are
at our most vulnerable point, then hurrying us along to clinch
the deal before we can consider all our options.

Such was the biblical case of Esau returning home after a
hard day's work, spent and famished. His need for instant
gratification won out over future goals that, at the time,
seemed esoteric. Let's face it, who would sit and ponder over
a birthright when his stomach was growling? And so Esau
made the first of several bad choices. After we make foolish
choices and realize later what they really cost, we have to
wonder who we are really angry at. Are we angry at the
person who we'd like to blame as the catalyst in our decision,
or are we upset at ourselves? I think that the anger we feel
toward ourselves is far more volatile than the anger we feel
toward others. Perhaps it is because it's hard to believe that
we could have ever been so foolish. Also, when we are angry
at others, we can punish them. We can avoid them. Give
them the silent treatment. Make them feel downright terrible
for what they've done. But when *we're* to blame, well, what
can we do?

Esau was weak, and Temptation met him at the place
where he likes to meet all of us—at our deepest point of
need or desire. This is the first place that Temptation strikes.
It doesn't take much to get the undisciplined to fold. Food,
sex, and money—these are the big three that get most of us
in trouble most of the time. No need for a lot of intricate foot-
work here. A simple waiting game is usually all that it takes
for the general populace to fall for the bait. With this in mind,
it's interesting to study Jacob in contrast to his brother Esau.
Jacob spent a lot of time considering the future. He knew
exactly what he wanted and where he was headed. He knew

these things, it seems, before he even came out of the womb. He started laying claim on what he wanted in the birth canal by trying to beat Esau out into the world. Some call it audacity, some call it healthy aggression.

Jacob wanted the rights of the firstborn. He wanted the blessing, and he was willing to do whatever it took to get it. Esau didn't give it much thought. He was occupied only with the present. He felt he had "a right" to what he wanted now. The Bible tells us that, "a person without self-control is as defenseless as a city with broken-down walls" (Proverbs 25:28 NLT), and that "a furious man aboundeth in transgression" (Proverbs 29:22 KJV). What's the connection between these two verses? Well, if we come to the understanding that anger is a reaction to what we feel are violated rights, we will see a common theme between the angry person and the person who lacks self-control—both have feelings of entitlement. Exactly what they are entitled to becomes the question.

Feelings of entitlement are dangerous because they leave us open to rationalizing why our immediate cravings should be satisfied with no thought of the consequences—that is, if any time is spent rationalizing at all. This is why it is important to surrender all rights to Christ. We must be of the mindset that it is "no longer I, but Christ in me" (see Galatians 2:20) that must be paid attention to. A dead man does not make demands. He is dead, as we are dead, in the sense that our lives are now supposed to be hidden in Christ. It is in the dying that all that we long for is gained.

I am reminded of the book I mentioned before entitled *Hope for the Flowers*, which told the tale of two caterpillars who longed to reach "the top." They had tremendous difficulty getting there. They physically exhausted themselves on the journey, then found themselves stuck in line waiting, barely inching forward, because those who had made it to "the top" were unwilling to lose their spot to make room for others striving to reach the same point. Sound familiar? Anyway, one of the caterpillars resigned itself to coming back down to earth and settling for a simpler life. One day that caterpillar encountered another caterpillar that was going through the process of metamorphosis. Here is where the caterpillar learned a powerful truth: "In order to reach the top, you must fly. And in order to be able to fly, you must be willing to die to everything." After all, a caterpillar has to shed its body in order to become a butterfly. Get it? You've got two choices—to remain earthbound, fleshbound, a servant of your desires, or to die so that you can fly. It's up to you and what you truly want.

Making a Stand

At some point in time we must develop a vision of what we ultimately want, and, like Jacob, be willing to make the moves or sacrifices necessary to possess the prize. We must have a single focus—tunnel vision, if you will—in order to stay on track. Otherwise we will become like the man who lacks self-control, standing for nothing and falling for everything, coming full circle to gain absolutely nothing in the end. We will then get caught up in a cycle of anger that further hinders our ability to make sound choices until we end up in a heap of despair.

We, like Paul, must determine to "lay aside every weight, and the sin which so easily ensnares us" (Hebrews 12:1 NKJV) and "press on towards the goal to win the prize for which God has called me heavenward in Christ Jesus" (Philippians 3:14 NIV). Yes, folks, there is a prize for overcoming. But first we must be willing to lay aside those sins and weights that bog us down, hang us up, and get us off the path. Weights can be people, stinkin' thinkin', doubts, circumstances, or situations that are not conducive to us moving ahead. I learned a long time ago that if I wanted to control my weight I couldn't keep a lot of sweets and snacks around my house. Whenever I have guests over, this always becomes a point of discussion because ultimately they will ask if I have something to nibble. Of course I do not. So the next question they ask is, "Why not?" To which I reply that I have no intention of looking like a beached whale, and that keeping tempting treats out of my kitchen is my safeguard to prevent this from happening.

The key to overcoming temptation is knowing yourself and dealing intelligently with that knowledge. Who are you fooling when you keep "nibbling" at the temptations of life? Temptation tries to lead you to believe that God is cruel, sitting on high and saying, "Look, but don't touch. Touch, but don't taste. Taste, but don't swallow," to quote Al Pacino's character, John Milton, in the movie *Devil's Advocate*. It's comments like this that really push our entitlement buttons. And off we go, carried away on a virtual feast of bingeing on our desires that leaves us sinsick and suffering from heartburn, massive regret, and indigestion. As we sit belching in disgust at our predicament, our little friend Temptation hunches his shoulders and says, "I only set the stage; you are the star in the act."

To Thine Own Self Be True

Esau's lackadaisical attitude toward his birthright set the stage for the further exploitation he experienced at the hands of Jacob. Perhaps his birthright was too vague a concept for him to grasp at the time. Therefore he never saw it as something important that he needed to protect. The bottom line was, Esau's present need for food spoke louder than his hopes for the future. Small wonder Jacob probably assumed he felt the same way about the blessing and went for it as well. He assumed that Esau's reaction would be pretty much the same indifference he had exhibited toward his birthright.

Imagine his surprise when Esau actually became upset this time—upset to the point of wanting to kill Jacob!

I'm sure at this point Jacob thought, *Now, wait a minute. Esau didn't care about his birthright; he exchanged it gladly for a bowl of soup. He hasn't cared about my parents' feelings in regard to the women he has chosen to marry. In fact, his wives have made them absolutely miserable. Obviously, Esau marches to his own beat, so he probably won't care about the blessing either. Besides, why should the blessing go to him and benefit foreign women anyway?* You see what happens when we miss what is important? Trust me, someone will be there to pick up the slack when you drop it. And that someone will be happy to get the blessing you miss.

Jacob knew two important things: He knew what was important in the long run, and he knew what he wanted. He went for it. He wanted the birthright and he got it. He wanted the blessing and he got it. He wanted Rachel and he got her. Not without a hitch, but that didn't stop him. Now, let me ask you this question: Do you know how important your birthright in Christ is? Satan knows. He's out to steal it. He doesn't like the idea that you, some mere little piece of puffed-up dust, have been given dominion over him. After all, he worked hard to become the Prince of Darkness. How dare you utter a simple prayer and get catapulted to a seat in the heavenly places with all authority over the enemy? He simply won't stand still for that!

Now consider this: Do you want to sacrifice your state of right-standing with God over a humbug, a bowl of soup? Whatever the temptation is, after you go through damage control, all it amounts to in the long run is the value of a bowl of soup. Another question: How important is the blessing to you? Is it important enough for you to hold out? Is it important enough not to displease your heavenly Father with the choice of people or things you join yourself to? Are you a Jacob or an Esau? Are you skimming the surface of life, just dealing with things at face value, or are you looking beyond where you stand, considering the big picture? Have you made a qualitative decision on what is really important in your life?

Jacob wanted certain things out of life. He knew he would need certain things in order to achieve what he wanted, so he was willing to make sacrifices. He ran for his life, worked fourteen years for the hand of Rachel....Think about it. He could have fallen prey to the temptation to become bitter when he got duped by Laban. Here he had worked for seven years without touching Rachel (and this had to be true, since he didn't know he had gotten Leah instead of Rachel on his wedding night), only to have his father-in-law pull a switch on him at the last minute. But Jacob swallowed that bitter pill and got right down to the business of doing whatever he had to do in order to get Rachel, and that involved working another seven years. And the Bible says that to Jacob, the seven years seemed as only a few days. That's how focused he was on what was important to him in the long run. He was so focused that he was willing to wrestle with an angel, refusing to let go until he had secured a blessing. You've got to have a serious depth of conviction in order to place demands on the supernatural!

Choosing the Path of Greater Resistance

Once you decide what is really important, Temptation must now choose another tactic—striking at your point of greatest fear. Therefore, you must have a do-or-die attitude about what is important. You cannot settle for the in-between. "If I perish, I perish," Esther said (see Esther 4:16). There was no turning back once she decided to risk her life for her people, even when Temptation whipped out a wonderful trinket to distract her. Now, I must admit that if I found myself in a perilous situation where the revelation of who I was could cost me my life, and I received the offer of half a kingdom before I had broached the subject of my dilemma, I think I would have had convenient amnesia when the king asked me, "Now, what was it you had to ask me?" I think I would have found myself saying, "Uh, you know...I can't remember for the life of me (pardon the pun) what I was going to say. Oh well, I guess it wasn't that important...so let's get back to that little discussion we were having about you giving me half of the kingdom. You were saying?"

But Esther was a better woman than I think I would have been in her situation. She stayed focused. Perhaps she knew that Temptation is always willing to bless us in order to bind us, to distract us, to make us break our stride and lose the blessing. Remember, "it is your Father's good pleasure to give you *the kingdom*" (Luke 12:32 KJV, emphasis added). The *whole* kingdom. Temptation wants to switch a half for the whole. Don't be fooled. This is why it is so important that we do not grow envious of the wicked, though they seem to get away with doing as they please and prosper in the midst of it. In reality, each "blessing" Temptation gives only leads them closer to everlasting separation from God.

How easy it would have been for Esther to take half the kingdom and forget about her people. How easily she could have languished behind the palace walls and hidden behind her status as queen. But she knew what was truly important—the preservation of her people. What is important for you to preserve? Ultimately, Esther not only preserved her people, but she also was rewarded with the spoils of the enemy. What does this mean to us? As we choose to preserve our holiness and our godly standards, our witness is preserved. When our witness is preserved, it affects the lives of those around us. We are rewarded with the spoils of the enemy. Lives that were lost are brought into the kingdom because we dared to be bold in revealing our identity and our stand to those who seemed to be in open opposition. In the realization of what hangs in the balance, we must ask ourselves if we are willing to say, "If our friendship perishes, it perishes"; or, "If this business deal perishes, it perishes"; or, "If my flesh perishes, it perishes."

As I fuse together several translations of this old familiar verse, it is evident that Paul said a mouthful when he gave these instructions: "Because of God's compassion, make a decisive dedication of your bodies, presenting all your members and faculties, as a living sacrifice, consecrated to God and worthy of His acceptance; this is the worship due from you as rational creatures, or, which is the worship it is right for you to give to Him" (see Romans 12:1). I think that's pretty self-explanatory, but for those of you who skate on the thin glaze of what you like to call the "permissive will of God," I must challenge you to first find a reference to the permissive will of God in Scripture. And second, you must confess that there is no such thing. The reality is that God has only one will with three levels—good, acceptable, and perfect. To suggest that He runs around with a backup "permissive" plan is to suggest that He is subject to the whims of men and angels, which is clearly not the case at all. He is a perfect God with a perfect plan that He has designed to unfold in perfect order.

Jesus encouraged us, "Be ye therefore perfect, even as your Father which is in heaven is perfect" (Matthew 5:48 KJV). God wants us to be mature Christians, grown-up, developed, in full stature—complete in Him. That is perfection. Perfection is not reached without sacrifice. Just ask any athlete. Perhaps that is why Paul likened living this life to training for an Olympic event. He talked about putting the body under, but here is where the problem arises. Discipline is what separates the pedestrians from those who go for the gold.

The Ultimate Example

If anyone understood what it took to stay focused on overcoming, it was Jesus Himself. He was "in all points tempted like as we are, yet without sin" (Hebrews 4:15 KJV). What was His secret? Well, He had several. First, He knew God intimately. He was one with the Father. Second, He knew who He was. He knew His position over the enemy. Third, He understood the reality of having an enemy. He knew who the enemy was and was not ignorant of his devices. Fourth, He was clear on His mission. For these reasons, Temptation knew that he could not deal with Jesus the same way he dealt with everyone else. His only hope was to attack Jesus at the heart of His identity, the seat of His ego. This is Temptation's last resort when all else fails. But Jesus, "who for the joy that was set before him endured the cross, despising the shame, and is set down at the right hand of the throne of God" (Hebrews 12:2 KJV).

Another one of my favorite lines from the movie *Devil's Advocate* is when John Milton, the devil, says, "Vanity, definitely my favorite sin." Temptation knows that when all else fails, he can usually count on our pride to rise to the occasion and insist on getting some respect and validation. Wrong move. "Pride goes before destruction, and a haughty spirit before a fall" (Proverbs 16:18 NKJV).

I recall being a new Christian and reading through the Scriptures, becoming so impressed with how cool Jesus was. Even in the hottest of situations, He maintained. When questioned, He never felt pressured to give an answer. As a matter of fact, in most instances He exchanged a question for a question. He was not interested in convincing anyone that He was "The Man." He, even more so than Daniel, maintained a flawless reputation. Unimpressed with the lust of the eyes, the lust of the flesh, or the pride of life, He looked neither to the right or to the left. He kept His eyes on the Father.

And when His accusers could find nothing to lay to His charge, they concocted fiction in order to condemn Him.

Rising Above the Press of the Flesh

Is it really possible to get to the place where Temptation cannot touch us? How do we get there? How do we get so tight with God that we bypass Temptation and his cronies? How do we get to a place where we're able to walk unharmed through the things that threaten to destroy the flesh, like when the people sought to throw Jesus off a cliff and He passed through the crowd untouched and went on His way? How do we get past the sting of death that sin brings?

What would make God send a chariot to pick you up as He did with Elijah? Think about it. Elijah is said to be a man of "like passion like us," but the man could pray powerful prayers. He walked in the prophetic office and declared that which God had pronounced was to come, and it unfolded just as he reported it. This was a man who prayed up a continuous flow of oil in the middle of a famine, called fire down from heaven, shut up the rain for three years and six months, prayed it back down, and kept on stepping, even when there was no evidence of a cloud in the sky. What type of relationship did Elijah have with God? What made God respond to the call of Elijah? What was it about Elijah's relationship with God that made him such a threat to the enemy? How do we get to the place of being on the *offense* rather than the *defense* against Temptation? Psalm 34:15 says, "The eyes of the LORD watch over those who do right; his ears are open to their cries for help" (NLT). Yet despite Elijah's great faith, we know that he suffered from fear, depression, and weariness just like we do. So what separates us from Elijah? Hold that thought for now, and let's move on.

I am intrigued that "Enoch walked with God: and he was not; for God took him" (Genesis 5:24 KJV). Can you imagine?

What kind of conversation were they having that day? Whatever it was, it got so good that God must have said—in Michelle paraphrase—"Enoch, you know I love talking with you. You need to just come on up here so we can finish talking."

Enoch bypassed the corruption of the flesh and went straight into the presence of God. What type of life did he live to warrant this wonderful experience? Hebrews 11:5 says that Enoch had the testimony that he pleased God. Jude tells of him prophesying of end times. Obviously, Enoch had a deeply intimate relationship with God. God told him of things to come and found him precious enough to translate into the heavens, lifting him above the circumstances of this world. Truly, Enoch did not adopt the standard of his forefather Cain; he offered the right sacrifice of worship to God—obedience and fellowship.

The common thread between Elijah, Enoch, and Jesus was that they walked in virtue—virtue as opposed to anointing. The anointing can come and go. As a matter of fact, your spiritual gifts can operate even when you're not submitted to God (imitating the anointing). Remember, "the gifts and callings of God are without repentance" (Romans 11:29 KJV). But virtue is a constant that one dwells in. Virtue is the inherent power that resides in a person by attributes of their nature. Purity, moral power, and excellence of soul separate believers from the masses and set them apart as overcomers. Virtue is the fruit of a life spent pursuing intimacy with God. Jesus was overflowing with virtue; it seeped out of Him and healed people who managed to touch even the hem of His garments. Demons cried out when He walked past. They had to leave; they could not remain in His presence. The closer we cleave to God, the less room the enemy has to occupy in our lives. The sound of God's heartbeat will drown out Satan's entreaties. Everything else pales in the light of God's presence.

And the more time we spend in His presence, the more evident it becomes to all within our circumference.

When Moses descended from Mount Sinai, where he had spent forty days and nights with the Lord, "his face was radiant because he had spoken with the LORD. When Aaron and all the Israelites saw Moses, his face was radiant, and they were afraid to come near him" (Exodus 34:29-30 NIV). The Bible goes on to say that Moses had to put a veil over his face, but whenever he entered the Lord's presence he removed the veil, and when he came out, the people saw that his face was radiant from being in the Lord's presence. My question to you is this: Can the enemy look at your face and see that you've been in the presence of the Lord? Is he afraid to come near you because the radiance of God's presence is all over you?

The Secret Place of Victory

I submit to you that intimacy with God is the secret place of overcoming the enemy and being ushered into the place of victory. When Moses went up on that mountain, he was serious in his quest for the fullness of God. He wanted to see God, and God allowed him to see just the back side of His glory—or His goodness—which was all that Moses could see and still survive in his human flesh. I find it interesting that flesh cannot survive in the face of God. We have now been given access through the blood of Jesus to come into the throne room of God, no longer having to settle for a glimpse of His back. We are privileged to stand before Him now in our prayer closets. If you've ever really pressed into that deep place of prayer and worship, then you know that flesh dies in the presence of God. This is when God can truly meet us and manifest His glory to us as He did with Moses. He made a covenant with Moses, and Moses worshiped Him.

There was interaction between man and his God, a two-sided conversation. This was the establishment of a deep and intimate friendship. No friendship is true friendship without transparency and covenant between both parties. These were the things that fixed Moses' heart and kept him from the temptation to wander in the wilderness. He chose to believe God in spite of what he could not see because of a relationship that had been sealed on the side of a mountain called Sinai. Moses had a promise he couldn't forget, a promise that screamed louder than any doubt or question Temptation could raise.

Many of us who struggle in our quest for holiness need to be encouraged. When our prayer lives suffer, we have an advocate who is diligently praying for us—Christ Jesus Himself. The cry of His heart concerning us is a precious one: "My prayer is not that you take them out of the world but that you protect them from the evil one. They are not of the world, even as I am not of it. Sanctify them by the truth; your word is truth.…Father, just as you are in me and I am in you. May they also be in us so that the world may believe that you have sent me. I have given them the glory that you gave me, that they may be one as we are one: I in them and you in me. May they be brought to complete unity to let the world know that you sent me and have loved them even as you have loved me. Father, I want those you have given me to be with me where I am, and to see my glory, the glory you have given me because you loved me before the creation of the world" (John 17:15-17,21-24 NIV).

Jesus wants us to make it! He knows and understands for Himself. And He prays for our protection. He prays that we will be sanctified by the Word. But how do we receive the Word that washes us? By stealing away as Jesus did in the early morning hours to commune with God, to worship, to rekindle the romance, the friendship with God. It's those early morning rendezvous that put the love light in our eyes to shoo away the enemy. As in any good romance, once is not enough. When the crowds pressed in and their voices grew too loud, Jesus stole away to a quiet place with God. In the cool of the evening, He sought His heavenly Father's face and shared the day with Him. It was this constant communion that kept Jesus grounded, kept Him clear, kept Him free to overcome Temptation.

I must interject here that I am rather concerned about the latest trend of prayer in some circles today. I find that many are storming into their prayer closets with a curt "hello" to God, then plunging into major warfare, ordering around the heavenlies like an army sergeant before stomping off to start their day. Sometimes I get a picture in my mind of God and the angels responding by putting their hands on their hips and saying, "Well, excuse us!"

How we've disintegrated to this, I'll never know. After all, Jesus gave us a very clear outline for prayer. It starts with entering into God's presence with worship, acknowledging who He is, then proceeding to pray about the things on God's heart—His kingdom agenda. We then are to follow this by asking for our personal daily provisions and forgiveness of our trespasses or debts. And finally we are to ask for protection against the devices of the enemy. I believe the enemy is listed last for a reason. First of all, the devil and his cohorts should never get more attention than God. I am an advocate of warfare because it is scriptural, but this is what sensitivity to the Holy Spirit is all about. "There is a time for everything...a time for war and a time for peace" (Ecclesiastes 3:1,8 NIV). As we pray, the Holy Spirit will assist us in prayer, alerting us to what we need to address. Throughout the Bible, people who entered into the presence of God received instruction. And that means that we need to spend as much time listening to God as we do talking to Him (or *at* Him).

Next, we do not need to yell at God. He can hear us. Just think of how you feel when someone yells at you. I don't think we even have to yell at the devil. I think he knows who means business. Many of us had mothers who only had to give us a certain look to get us to settle down. That look was lethal; it held the silent promise of much misery if we proceeded any further in our disobedience.

A policeman puts up his hand in traffic without saying a word, and cars screech to a halt. Get the picture? True authority is wielded by an understanding of position. There is a time when a shout is called for and effective, but I think this is the exception rather than the rule. The devil is no fool. He understands the authority of the believer, and he knows if you're "packing," as they say in the streets. (That means you've got artillery on your person.) In the book of Acts, the demons said they knew Paul and they knew Jesus, but they knew they didn't have to take the brothers of Sceva seriously. The devil only feels threatened by those who are intimate with God. He knows that anyone who is friends with God is a dangerous foe. Is your name on the devil's list of people to avoid?

How to Get Your Heart's Desire

I think the church has worked out all kinds of formulas to deal with sin and temptation because the real formula seems too simple. We like to work. If we labor, we feel we've really done something. So we bind, we loose, we cast down, we uproot, we tear down, we nullify, we destroy, we war, and we fight without ever getting our instructions from the One who has a bird's-eye view of the battle. Didn't Jesus promise to send the Holy Spirit to guide us and teach us? To say this is the way, walk ye in it? If God's Word is the thing that sheds light on how to live victoriously day to day (and this is why we ask for daily bread), how do we get that Word? By spending time with Him, by conversing with Him, by placing our ear against His heart. Intimacy with Him releases the impartation we need to overcome the wiles of the enemy. In that prayer closet, He reveals the schemes against us that the enemy has up his sleeve. He lets us know what to look out for, what to do, what to say, and how to deal with every situation we may encounter.

While people run daily to psychics to have their fortune told, we have access to the One who knows all things and shares information freely with those who seek His face. He longs to bless us, to free us, to promote us, to give us the desires of our hearts. And "the blessing of the LORD brings wealth, and he adds no trouble to it" (Proverbs 10:22 NIV). Temptation distracts you from the way that leads to receiving all that you desire.

Job 22:21-30 says, "Submit to God and be at peace with him; in this way prosperity will come to you. Accept instruction from his mouth and lay up his words in your heart. If you return to the Almighty, you will be restored: If you remove wickedness far from your tent and assign your nuggets to the dust, your gold of Ophir to the rocks in the ravines, then the Almighty will be your gold, the choicest silver for you. Surely then you will find delight in the Almighty and will lift up your face to God. You will pray to him, and he will hear you, and you will fulfill your vows. What you decide on will be done, and light will shine on your ways. When men are brought low and you say, 'Lift them up!' then he will save the downcast. He will deliver even one who is not innocent, who will be delivered through the cleanness of your hands" (NIV).

Now that is powerful! If you submit to God and do things His way—walking in righteousness and holiness with Him— you will be blessed with prosperity. That's not a bad deal, but it doesn't end there. If you really listen to what God says and return to Him, you will be restored. Restoration speaks of *all* that you've lost—opportunities, relationships, things, hopes, dreams. If you toss off all the things that you held so dear and precious and make the Lord as precious as you once found those things to be, you can lift up your face to God and ask for anything, and He will hear you.

Why will He hear you? Because your desires will be transformed, and you will be praying out of the heart of God as it beats in you. You will desire what He desires and find joy in what He finds joy in. He will bless you with the blessing of Elijah, the ability to "decree a thing, and it shall be established unto thee" (Job 22:28 KJV). You will be able to fulfill your vows of being obedient to the Lord, keeping all those promises that you make when you're feeling strong. You will be able to pray for others and effectively intercede for people, even for those who are not innocent in the sight of the Lord. God will be able to use you as a vessel to glorify Him in the sight of sinners because you will walk in power. Others will seek you out to pray for them because they know you can get a prayer through. In short, our tendency is to negotiate with Temptation for the things we think we want when our time would be better spent yielding to God's direction, which ultimately opens the door for Him to provide true fulfillment in our lives. If only we spent more time talking with God and less time giving audience to Temptation, well, the possibilities would be endless!

Finishing the Race

In Hannah Hurnard's wonderful allegory *Hind's Feet on High Places,* the main character, Much Afraid, longs to go to the High Places with the Shepherd. He consents to her taking the journey and, to Much Afraid's horror, offers her two companions, Sorrow and Suffering. But there is a comfort in holding their hands. They actually strengthen her to endure

the trek. Along the way, Pride, Fear, and several other char-
acters follow her to throw her off-course and make her turn
back. As she allows them to distract her with their taunts, she
drops the hands of her companions and wanders off into
dangerous places, getting lost and finding herself in difficulty.

Much Afraid eventually has to grasp the hands of Sorrow
and Suffering once again in order to continue her trip. Each
time she goes through this exercise, she experiences pain
afresh. But eventually she learns to shut out the voices of
those who continually taunt her, letting go of all that she
holds dear. Sorrow and Suffering become Peace and Joy and
she is transformed into Grace and Glory. God will allow us to
continue our conversations with Temptation until we learn,
through our own trial and error, that Temptation is our
enemy.

Temptation offers us a shortcut that leads to a dead end,
while God encourages us to take a journey that leads to
blessings that cannot be taken away. Unfortunately, we
sometimes grow lazy. And when this happens, we pick the
seemingly easiest option. But every time we take the hand of
Temptation, we find ourselves limping back to the cross, discouraged and broken. Yes, "sin is pleasurable for a season."
It can be exhilarating, and exciting, but the end is always the
same—a crash landing complete with scars and festering
wounds.

It's time to get off the merry-go-round and make a qualitative decision to walk in virtue, in intimate fellowship with
God, circumspect reverence before an Almighty King, to
walk the walk of complete and undivided worship. It is only
then that we will be able to repeat the words of Paul: "I
have fought the good fight, I have finished the race, I have
kept the faith. Now there is in store for me the crown of
righteousness, which the Lord, the righteous Judge, will

award to me on that day" (2 Timothy 4:7-8 NIV). This is only the beginning of the reward for those who overcome. There's something to be said for being able to embrace the satisfaction of looking back on a job well done.

GOD IS FAITHFUL!

"What shall we say, then? Shall we go on sinning so
that grace may increase? By no means! We died to
sin; how can we live in it any longer?"

ROMANS 6:1 NIV

THERE ARE CERTAIN FACTS THAT CANNOT be ignored as we
take one last look at a subject that has intrigued us from the
beginning of time. We have a very real enemy who takes
advantage of our heart condition. Nothing has really changed
in Satan's *modus operandi*. Temptation still has the same old
rap he had in the beginning. I think that sometimes this is
where we get in trouble. We get lulled into the sameness of
what he does, and we fail to recognize him as the culprit who
introduces us to trouble. We keep expecting him to come at
us with some new tactic, but instead he keeps hammering
away with the same old hammer. While we're looking for
him to sneak up on us from the left, he tiptoes up to our right
and throws us off guard. The verdict? Never underestimate
this enemy. He is powerful, highly intelligent, and most
subtle. Furthermore, he has been studying you a lot longer
than you have been studying him.

More importantly, never overlook the power of the flesh and the tendencies of your own heart. The moment you think more highly of yourself than you ought, you set yourself up for a serious fall. You must watch yourself, lock all your doors, and seal all your hatches. You must be ever alert not to "give place to the devil" (Ephesians 4:27 KJV). Even though Satan is a powerful entity, he needs you in order to fulfill his agenda. Why is he seeking to devour you? Because you hold something most precious—his way of entry into the earth realm. The spirit needs a house—a body—in order to translate his influence into action. This is why Jesus wants us to yield our bodies as living sacrifices so that we can become living translations of the Word of God. After His ascension into heaven, He promised to send a Comforter and Teacher. Now the Holy Spirit fills believers in order to manifest God's power in the earth. The fight for your body as a host is a serious one in the spirit realm. This is why Paul urged us to be "filled with the Spirit" (Ephesians 5:18 NIV). This safeguards us against yielding our bodies to works of unrighteousness.

God's grace is really the gift of power to manifest Him, which means that the choice to say yea or nay to Temptation is totally ours. The enemy cannot strong-arm us. As I said earlier, in a court of law, Temptation merely would be named an accessory to the crime of sin. You would be charged as the guilty offender. It is crucial that we "be very careful, then, how [we] live—not as unwise but as wise, making the most of every opportunity, because the days are evil. Therefore do not be foolish, but understand what the Lord's will is" (Ephesians 5:15-17 NIV). We are also told to "be imitators of God" (verse 1) and "have nothing to do with the fruitless deeds of darkness" (verse 11).

I once wrote a song called "No Regrets" that was about lessons I had learned in my lifetime. In it, I reflected, "I have to say I've had some private wars to fight, with vocal enemies like my wounded pride, I've made my peace within, denied my heart of pleasantries I knew would waste my time." Perhaps it's age, perhaps it's the passage of time, or perhaps it's just growing weary of suffering the consequences. Eventually we must finally come to the end of ourselves and decide enough is enough. How long will we avoid the responsibility of taking care of ourselves? That is what it boils down to. Every instruction that comes from the lips of God is for our own good, to promote our own well-being.

The greater questions we must ask ourselves are these: How much do we love God? How much do we love ourselves? How much do we love our neighbor? After all, Jesus did say that all of the other commandments hung on the first two. "Love the Lord your God with all your heart and with all your soul and with all your mind and with all your strength" (Mark 12:30 NIV). Love the Lord from the center of your will, with your entire inner man. Let your love for Him permeate your thought life and affect even your discipline. Sometimes it takes all your strength to hang on to your love for God in the midst of hard times. In spite of it all, we must persevere in our love for God. This is the first and greatest commandment. And the second is like it: "'Love your neighbor as yourself.' All the Law and the Prophets hang on these two commandments" (Matthew 22:39-40 NIV). There you have it. Obedience is not something to be done out of duty; it is an act of love.

How can I love God and then do things that hurt and offend Him? How can I love my neighbor and then not work in their best interest? How can I love myself and do things that endanger the soundness of my own mind and body? In this sense, people slowly commit suicide every day. When I run into people I went to school with, I am initially shocked at how weary some of them now look. Sin takes its toll on us physically, as well as spiritually and emotionally. It shows. It ages us prematurely. It puts pressure on our vital organs. Sin hurts. Sin is ugly. But it's sneaky; you coast along, having a good time, and then all of a sudden, seemingly out of nowhere, *bam!* You find yourself breathless from its blow. That is Satan's intention—to draw the breath of God, that element which made you a living soul, out of you. He wants to leave you gasping for air, unable to worship, because you're too busy trying to survive the effects of your predicament.

Pain, disappointment, deferred hope, and bitterness are weeds guaranteed to choke out worship. Guilt will keep you out of the garden, period. It is the traitor that dwells in the gates, jangling the keys he has stolen from you, telling you that you are unworthy to possess the keys to your own deliverance. Don't believe him. God is faithful to forgive. Chastising yourself for being foolish is only necessary when you refuse to learn your lesson. The revelation gained from a fall can be worth its weight in gold if grasped. So we learn to "rejoice in our sufferings, because we know that suffering produces perseverance; perseverance, character; and character hope. And hope does not disappoint us" (Romans 5:3-5 NIV).

What does this mean to those who struggle with Temptation? It means that even if learning through tribulation is not our favorite style of learning, it can still work to our benefit because we will eventually discover that sin is not worth it. The short time of pleasure does not compensate for the aftereffects. Therefore, we learn to become patient and wait on God to meet our desires. As we give God room to manifest His faithfulness to us, we gain the knowledge that He is faithful to deliver. And His way always turns out better than the temporary fix that we were considering. Waiting on God builds up our faith and gives us hope. As long as we have hope that God will fulfill us in every way, we won't do things that cause us to be ashamed because our love for God will overrule the desires of our flesh. Romans 5:6 says, "You see, at just the right time, when we were still powerless, Christ died for the ungodly" (NIV). Another translation says, "When we were still powerless to help ourselves..."[17] and another says, "When we were utterly helpless with no way of escape...."[18]

"God is faithful; he will not let you to be tempted beyond what you can bear. But when you are tempted, he will also provide a way out so that you can stand up under it. Therefore, my dear friends, flee from idolatry..." (1 Corinthians 10:13-14 KJV). There you have it. A clause like that doesn't leave much room for excuses. God will actually pave the way for you to make a clean getaway when Temptation corners you. *And* He will let the adversary tempt you only within the realm of what He knows you can resist! Now that's deep. So what is this? Is it all a setup? No. God, in His fairness, will not allow you to be overwhelmed. He knows your limitations, but He also wants you to exercise your holiness muscles and set your own boundaries. He wants you to become a mature Christian, not a robot. In the book of Judges, the Lord allowed the enemy to remain among the Israelites to teach them warfare and to test their hearts to see if they would be obedient to Him (see Judges 3:1-4). Temptation reveals the state of your heart toward God. Anything you just have to have is an idol. So rejoice when one is uncovered, and shatter it. You've been empowered to do so.

Finally, remember that you are not dealing with mere flesh and blood, but with supernatural beings. "We wrestle not against flesh and blood, but against principalities, against powers, against the rulers of the darkness of this world, against spiritual wickedness in high places" (Ephesians 6:12 KJV). The enemy has assigned a special task force to infiltrate your world and bring you down. Therefore, you need to keep yourself covered. The armor of God is a sure defense. Truth will always diffuse the most well-crafted lie. It will keep your wits in place. Righteousness will keep your heart secure. The gospel will keep you from stumbling or turning aside; it will be a lamp unto your feet. Faith will stop every dart of doubt and extinguish every question and every fear. And salvation will be your crowning glory, keeping you in sound mind. The Word of God will cut through everything that is not sound and lay it bare. These are essential garments for every believer. Those who fight in the flesh will not be able to stand. This is why Temptation likes to draw so much attention to the flesh. He knows if he can get you to focus on the cravings of the flesh, he can pull you out of the spirit. Therefore, strive to always "walk in the Spirit, and you shall not fulfill the lust of the flesh" (Galatians 5:16 NKJV).

So you have an enemy? You're not alone. But remember that you have an intercessor, a partner in the battle, one who watches over you with a jealous love and fights on your behalf! You also have been given "authority...over all the power of the enemy, and nothing shall by any means hurt you" (Luke 10:19 NKJV). No weapon Satan has devised will prosper against you! You have been given the keys to the kingdom, and the power to bind and loose (see Matthew 16:19). Satan is like a little boy jumping up and down as you hold the keys above your head. "Give them to me!" he shouts. Let this knowledge empower you. You hold the keys to the kingdom—your own righteousness, peace, and joy in the Holy Ghost. Jesus has handed them to you. Rise to the occasion. Grasp them with a vengeance. Jesus has overcome the world, and because of Him "ye are of God, little children, and have overcome them: because greater is he that is in you, than he that is in the world" (1 John 4:4 KJV). So when Temptation offers you the world, tell him he can have it. "Love not the world, neither the things that are in the world" (1 John 2:15 KJV). After all, everything the eye can see is temporary. Turn instead heavenward...and worship.

NOTES

1. TCNT is The Twentieth Century New Testament (Old Tappan, NJ Fleming H. Revell, 1904). Beck is An American Translation (Coudersport, PA: Leader Publishing Co., 1976).

2. See *The Holy Bible: A Translation from the Latin Vulgate in the Light of the Hebrew and Greek Originals* (New York: Sheed and Ward, Inc., 1981).

3. "Disobedience" from *When We Were Very Young* by A.A. Milne, illustrations by E.H. Shephard. Copyright © 1924 by E.P. Dutton, renewed 1952 by A.A. Milne. Used by permission of Dutton Children's Books, a division of Penguin Putnam, Inc.

4. Karen C. Hinckley, *Story of Stories* (Colorado Springs, CO: NavPress, 1991).

5. See *The Holy Bible: The Berkeley Version in Modern English* by Gerrit Verkuyl (Grand Rapids: Zondervan Publishing House, 1945).

6. See *The New English Bible* (Oxford: Oxford University Press, 1961).

7. See *Living Prophecies* by Ken Taylor (Wheaton, IL: Tyndale House Publishers, 1966).

8. "When I Look into Your Holiness," by Wayne and Cathy Perrin. Copyright © 1981 Integrity's Hosanna! Music/ASCAP. All rights reserved. International copyright secured. Used by permission. c/o Integrity Music, Inc., 1000 Cody Road, Mobile, AL 36655.

9. See *The New American Bible* (Washington, D.C.: Confraternity of Christian Doctrine, 1970).

10. Ibid.

11. Ibid.

12. See *The Holy Bible: A Translation from the Latin Vulgate.*

13. Ibid.

14. Ibid.

15. See *A New Translation of the Bible* by James Moffatt (New York: Harper & Row, Inc., 1954).

16. See *Living Prophecies* by Ken Taylor.

17. See *The Holy Bible: A Translation from the Latin Vulgate.*

18. See *Living Letters* by Ken Taylor (Wheaton, IL· Tyndale House Publishers, 1962).

RECOMMENDED READING

The Battle Is the Lord's, Tony Evans, Moody Press

The Bondage Breaker, Neil T. Anderson, Harvest House Publishers

Deliver Me, Richard Exley, Thomas Nelson Publishers

The Handbook for Spiritual Warfare, Dr. Ed Murphy, Thomas Nelson Publishers

Living with Your Passions, Erwin W. Lutzer, Victor Books

The Serpent of Paradise, Erwin W. Lutzer, Moody Press

Spiritual Authority, Watchman Nee, Christian Fellowship Publications

The Spiritual Man, Watchman Nee, Christian Fellowship Publications

The Three Battlegrounds, Francis Frangipane, Advancing Church Publications

The Way of Holiness, Stephen F. Olford, Crossway Books

OTHER BOOKS BY
MICHELLE MCKINNEY HAMMOND

If you would like to correspond with Michelle, you can write her c/o:

HeartWing Ministries
P.O. Box 11052
Chicago, IL 60611
or email her at **heartwingmin@yahoo.com**

For newsletters and ministry updates log on to:
www.heartwing.org
or **www.mckinneyhammond.com**

For information on scheduling
speaking engagements contact:
Speak Up Speaker Services at 888-870-7719